Sisters in Blood

Wensley Clarkson

Published by Blake Publishing Ltd,
3 Bramber Court, 2 Bramber Road,
London W14 9PB, England

First published in 2002

ISBN 18578247 X

British Library Cataloguing-in-Publication Data:
A catalogue record for this book is available
from the British Library.

Typeset by t2

Printed in Great Britain by Bookmarque

1 3 5 7 9 10 8 6 4 2

Papers used by John Blake Publishing Limited are natural, recyclable products made from wood grown in sustainable forests. The manufacturing processes conform to the environmental regulations of the country of origin.

Contents

Dear Reader,

The tales contained within these pages are not for the faint-hearted. They are the stories of some of the most extreme, bloody crimes committed by women. Some will astonish you with their violence and rage; some with their cold, calculating evil; and others with the depths of misery that led their lives down a path of terrible destruction.

Expect all the things that you would least expect of the fairer sex. For here are the true stories of what happens when human emotion can no longer be reigned in, when passion can no longer be controlled.

Witness the schoolteacher who took schoolboys and taught them to kill; or the housewife who used sex to bend the minds of mental patients to murder; or the nurse who took care of her patients to a permanent and fatal level.

These women are from every walk of life, a collection as diverse as they are deadly. Some loners, some seemingly respectable and others possessed of a sinister logic and yet all are united as 'Sisters in Blood'.

James Ravenscroft
Editor
Blake's True Crime Library

A Free Trip to God

A strange silence shrouded the grounds of the Lainz General Hospital. It was as if there was no air. Nothing moved. None of the many trees swayed. No one walked in the grounds. The grey, crumbling faade of the main building contrasted with the pretty apple blossoms dotted throughout the five acres of grassland surrounding the hospital.

Huge ferns cast great shadows on the ornate 150-year-old mansion that had long ago been converted into a centre for the sick and elderly. There was so little sign of life from the outside. So much silence. So much expectation.

The vast gothic windows appeared almost black from the outside. The five storey property looked far taller than it really was. It could have been ten or even fifteen storeys. It had that sort of imposing effect when people visited.

Atop the main frontage were gargoyles – a set of six of them staring intently down on all who entered. A piece of masonry just next to their footage had once crashed down in front of a group of elderly patients. Perhaps it was time for them to leave?

The place exerted a strange emotional pull on anyone who happened to be passing. The sheer enormity of the building. Its long, drawn out features. The lichen-encrusted statues built into virtually every corner. The once pale stonework darkened by a century and a half of grime. Up one side, clumps of ivy dung desperately to powdery mortar.

If it had ever been given the maintenance it deserved, then the Lainz could have maintained its original splendour. It had all the classic ingredients to be pronounced a building of great historical value, but the general public tended to keep well away. A place full of the dying and elderly was hardly going to become a tourist attraction. There was something about it that made the locals suspicious. An aura of death hung constantly around it. Poor souls waiting out their last days in morbid, hopeless circumstances.

When people drove past, it would catch their eye. But only for a second. You wouldn't want to stare too long. All the same, the people of Vienna knew the Lainz General Hospital well. It regularly starred in their news bulletins and featured in the newspapers. But that did not stop it becoming a place to avoid.

Inside, however, it was full of typical, prim Austrian efficiency. The high-ceilinged rooms helped the light pour into every corner. It was clean but the paintwork had certainly seen better days. The walls and corridors had a slightly off white sheen with the occasional damp stain here and there, like a record of all the residents who had come and gone over the years.

The worst thing, though, was the silence.

Of course there were noises. Elevators opening and closing. Trolleys being pushed along the shiny, patent floors. But there was no hum of people. No friendly voices. No childish laughter.

It was like a barrier that hit everyone who entered that place. First they would be struck by the emptiness in the grounds, then they would be taken completely aback by the lack of voices inside. It was not as if there were no people around. There were nurses, auxiliaries, and porters everywhere. Scurrying up and down the corridors on endless errands. But no one stopped and smiled. No one uttered a word. And where were the patients? That eerie silence was the biggest reminder of all. Where were the patients?

A cold, bleak darkness fell on the Lainz General Hospital one day in February 1989. As the day shift staff moved off to their homes in the nearby suburbs they were replaced by the night workers. The men and women whose lives somehow adapted to those strange nocturnal habits. Many of them held together whole families despite the fact they were starting work when most people are thinking about bed.

By midnight at the Lainz, that daytime silence had been completely replaced by an even more sinister atmosphere. Now the sounds of the elevators, the trolleys, and the errands had long gone. But nothing had taken their place. Every now and again a cough or a splutter broke it. But the sound proof doors would smother it, like a hand over the mouth. No one but the chosen few could possibly know what was going on.

You could walk each and every corridor in the hospital and learn nothing about the patients. They might as well not have existed and since 80% of the residents of the Lainz were over seventy years of age, it was unclear if anyone really cared.

Most of the doctors had long gone. They tended to work a five day week like any good office worker. Few of them even appeared at weekends.

Sickness could wait. If it was an emergency one of the housemen could cope – even though he (or she) may have only just medically qualified. It seemed ironic that the most dire cases ended up being dealt with by the least experienced doctors.

And that attitude was starting to drift through to the nurses. Fewer and fewer of them wanted to work those gruelling night shifts. They were happy to hand over control of the wards to the teams of lowly paid auxiliaries – the men and women who wanted to be nurses but failed to pass (or take) the necessary exams. It was not really the right way to run things, but the system prevailed at the Lainz and no one really seemed to care.

The silence grew.

Auxiliary nurse Waltraud Wagner was more than happy to take on the additional responsibilities. The fewer bossy nurses patrolling her ward at the hospital the better. The night shifts were bad enough but if you ended up with some Sgt. Major breathing down your neck it would have been intolerable.

In fact, Waltraud rather enjoyed her job as a result. She had much more power and influence than she could reasonably have expected and she was allowed to just get on with her work on the ward – known as Pavilion 5.

Back home, husband Willi hardly inspired her. He demanded food and sex – in that order – most evenings before she left for work. But she really did not feel in the mood at that sort of time. Her favourite moments for passion came late at night or really early in the morning – but Willi was never around then.

Still, Waltraud understood her husband's frustrations. After all, she was his wife and they had once enjoyed a good sex life. It was just so difficult to explain to Willi. As far as he was concerned, the moment she put on that nursing uniform it was an invitation to lust. But it was nearly always at the wrong time. In any case, she couldn't go to work with a crumpled, messy uniform.

So, over time, as the grind of a night-shift life became ingrained in her system, Waltraud found other ways of satisfying herself.

Julia Drapal had been quite a ballerina star in her day. During the 1950s she had performed at the Vienna Royal Ballet time and time again. Kings, Queens, Presidents – they had all seen her dance.

In Austria, she was as famous as Margot Fonteyn had been in Britain. Julia had been a very privileged person during that period. Chauffeur driven limousines would take her and her husband everywhere. They dined out at the most expensive restaurants. They travelled the world. It was a marvellous time. And it was those very memories that were now keeping Julia alive.

Her frail body had failed her once too often in the previous few years and now she had become a patient at the Lainz General Hospital. She hated it there. But there had been little choice in the matter. The doctors had told her husband she needed full-time medical care. He could no longer cope. She had to be looked after.

But, like anyone who once received the adulation of millions, Julia was not an easy person to deal with. She had been used to people attending to her every whim. Now she was just another number on a clipboard at the end of her cast iron bed. Her hatred for the hospital and all it represented manifested itself in her attitude towards the staff. In short, she was a cantankerous woman. Given to bursts of insults and bad temper.

Sometimes she would push the nurses away when they tried to tend to her. On other occasions she would try to degrade them by referring to them as 'common people'.

Julia was not exactly the most popular patient on Pavilion 5.

'Time for mouth wash.'

No elderly patient had the energy to refuse when Waltraud Wagner issued orders. Some of the old men rather liked her dominant, strong-willed manner. With her large, round eyes, she certainly looked an attractive proposition to some of those patients. Her uniform always seemed to hug her body in just the right places and those black, regulation stockings – well …

But not many of those old men would ever consider actually getting fresh with Waltraud to her face. However, that didn't stop them fantasising about what she might do to them if ever she caught them.

And Waltraud knew full well that some of the men on Pavilion 5 had crude thoughts about her. She didn't mind. In fact, she found it quite flattering. But she did get annoyed when they occasionally tried to molest her.

There was the time the old gentleman in bed number 12 complained of having trouble passing water. When Waltraud arrived at his bedside, he insisted she hold his penis while he tried to urinate. For a few moments, Waltraud obliged until she realised what that dirty old man was really up to. Some of the other auxiliaries used to gossip about seducing the patients.

'I'd marry one of those old sods if they promised to leave me all their money,' said one of Waltraud's colleagues.

She was appalled.

'Oh. I could never do it with an old guy. I don't mind what they are thinking about me but to let them touch me. Uggh. Now if they were under 50 that would be a different matter …'

Waltraud had her own strange set of standards in life and they were just as inconsistent as everyone else's.

'Come on now Julia. It is mouthwash time.'

Time to get down to business. Julia Drapal was a bloody annoying patient. Only a few days earlier the old boot had called her a 'common slut' when she had tried to change her bedclothes.

She had decided then and there that Julia definitely needed a mouthwash but she needed a colleague to help her administrate the 'treatment'.

Irene Leidolf tended to work closely with Waltraud because they were two of the youngest auxiliaries on Pavilion 5. At 27, Irene was also a fairly attractive sight compared with many of the other thick set auxiliaries, most of whom were in their late 40s and early 50s. She was much shyer than Waltraud though. She rarely joined in with the gossipy chats they frequently all enjoyed on the ward. But Waltraud liked her because she did as she was told. Irene never questioned any order.

'Come on Irene. Help me give her the mouthwash.' It was midnight in Pavilion 5, but quite a few of the elderly patients were awake. They watched as the two burly nurses approached Julia's bedside.

It was not a pleasant sight.

Those frail and withered people were about to witness what they lived in fear of receiving themselves – the dreaded mouthwash treatment. No one knew why it was administered. But they were well aware that it always brought things to an abrupt ending.

Waltraud put a heavily stained plastic glass filled with water to Julia's lips. They would not open.

'Come on Julia. It's mouthwash time. You know

you must have your mouthwash. Now come on. Open up.'

Julia was having none of it. She had watched enough beds empty in the previous few months to know that this was not a treatment she wished to receive.

'Right. Hold her down!' Waltraud barked at her younger colleague Irene. 'Come on. We must get this one done.'

She always referred to the patients as if they were more like cows in line for a branding than human beings. Waltraud pinched Julia's nose closed with her thumb and her index finger.

Suddenly a look of complete horror glazed across the old lady's face. Her gaunt cheeks and sagging neck line seemed to stiffen with anxiety. Her eyes were wide open now. Desperately searching for someone to intervene. She tried to move her arms up to ward off the nurse but Irene had both her wrists locked tight.

'Now. You will take the mouthwash won't you Julia.'

There was absolutely no doubt in Waltraud's voice. She knew exactly what she was doing and that made it all the more terrifying for her victim.

As the water slithered down Julia's throat, she tried to cough it back up. For a split second she succeeded in arresting the flow. But the effort proved too much to sustain and her lungs surrendered to the cascade of water that was now pouring down her gullet.

Julia's eyes tried to catch Waltraud. They tried to appeal to her to stop. But Waltraud had deliberately blanked her expression. She was staring at the wall behind the bed. She did not want any emotion to impinge on the horrifying reality.

The only noise that could now be heard was the slight gurgle when Waltraud forced too much water too quickly down her patient's throat. She responded by slowing down slightly. It was imperative that the water filled those lungs to bursting point. It would not be long now. It would not be long.

Irene Leidolf stood there holding down this frail old lady without really giving any thought to what she was doing. She had a family to feed and she wasn't going to put her job on the line by refusing to help Waltraud. In any case, Julia's time had come. It was as simple as that. Her attitude was no different to the guards at Auschwitz. It came as second nature to follow orders. Why question them and upset the apple cart. Life had to go on ... for some.

Waltraud had by now emptied the entire contents of that glass of water down Julia's throat. She released her hold on her tiny, limp nose.

'There. That wasn't so bad was it?'

If Julia had had the energy to speak she would have cursed Waltraud to a thousand deaths. Instead, she knew her own demise was imminent.

As Waltraud walked back towards her desk she turned to Irene and said: 'There. That's another one who has got a free trip to God.'

Coughing and spluttering, Julia could feel the darkness setting in. The pain in her lungs was so great it was as if someone had forced an iron bar down their entire length. Her arms were no longer being held down by Irene, but they might as well have been. There was no strength left in them. Her head slumped to one side and she stared out along the ward to where Waltraud and Irene were sitting. They seemed to be sharing a private joke. Maybe they were talking about her? She realised with a jolt of finality, that she would never be able to find out.

The pain in her lungs was awful. A stabbing sensation had taken over now. Breathing seemed like a great labour, something unnatural to her body. She just wanted the agony to end.

As the last few minutes of her life ticked away, her thoughts of fighting and her sense of survival were all but fading. Julia had lost her last battle, and cursed her last nurse.

'It's one of the patients. I think she's dead.'

Some hours had passed since Waltraud had administered her mouthwash treatment. Now Waltraud was telling the duty doctor that his services were required.

'I'll be there in about thirty minutes. There's hardly any point in rushing.'

Pronouncing a patient dead was not exactly classified as an emergency in a hospital like the Lainz. In any case, water in the lungs was a common contributory cause of death amongst the elderly. The doctor would not even raise an eyebrow at the discovery of the liquid. Waltraud knew. She had done it so many times before.

Waltraud then casually drew the curtains around Julia's bedside. Ironically, it was that very action which told the other patients they had lost another resident. If those curtains had never been drawn, probably they would never have known. But now it was being advertised in vivid detail. Another desperately needed bed for another hopeless case. For most of the patients who entered Pavilion 5 had little or no chance of survival. Waltraud Wagner and her colleagues would see to that.

Waltraud was troubled by one aspect of this deadly scenario – why did she enjoy it so much? Each time she snuffed the life out of yet another Pavilion 5 patient it prompted a surge of satisfaction. A feeling that made her immensely proud. Maybe it was something to do with the power it gave her? Or perhaps she actually felt like a true angel of mercy – putting all those bleak, worn lives to rest for ever?

The afterglow would stay with her for hours after a killing. She would arrive home at her flat at six in the morning elated by the horrendous act she had just committed.

'How was work darling?', her husband would ask innocently through his sleepy haze.

'Oh. Fine', she would reply. Waltraud could hardly describe her working night as an auxiliary nurse as 'wonderful' to her husband, but that was precisely how she felt. A radiance would illuminate her soul.

It was at moments like that she would give her husband the sex he had craved for most the previous nights. Often, Waltraud would not bother taking her uniform off – she knew he liked it that way.

Unbuttoning the front of her tunic and exposing her breasts would be enough for him to know what she wanted.

'It's so easy. And they'll never know we did it.'

Waltraud Wagner was enjoying a rare evening out at a local beer cellar with her co-conspirators Irene Leidolf, Maria Gruber and Stephanie Mayen.

The four women had decided they deserved a night on the town – after all they had managed to murder nearly fifty patients over the previous five years. The truth was they had stopped counting long ago. The numbers really began to increase after Waltraud devised her mouthwash treatment. That was so much easier than injecting huge amounts of insulin.

Stephanie was far older than the other three and seemed to fit the role of a ferocious, bulky auxiliary far better than her younger colleagues.

Yet, ironically, she was the more hesitant member of this self-professed chapter of the Angels of Death. Maria – a heavy set women in her early 50's – was appalled when she first realised what was happening. But then Waltraud started to convince her they were doing all these elderly, infirm patients a favour.

'In any case. Some of them are so bloody annoying they deserve it.'

Chilling words from the ringleader. But the other women were not about to argue with her. They were all in this together.

In that lively basement beer cellar that night, the four women were off duty for once. There would be no distant cries in the night. No incontinent old men. No senile dementia. For once, they were together outside work – and they were determined to have a good time.

When Irene and Waltraud caught the eye of two businessmen types in the far corner of the cellar, they returned their glances provocatively. These women were out to enjoy themselves after many months tolling in the killing fields of Lainz General Hospital.

The beer and wine flowed freely as did the talk that evening. As usual Waltraud was the one holding court. She craved for attention wherever she was. In the hospital she loved the fear she induced among the more timid patients. She relished in her display of power over them. She could decide whether they lived or died. It was an amazing feeling.

It was exactly the same in that bar cellar. She wanted to be the one in charge. She would love to look at all their attentive faces lapping up every word she uttered. She knew she had them under her spell.

She decided to put them all to a little test. A way to see just how loyal they really were.

'None of you ever say much about what we have done. Why not? Are you not proud of the fact we have put those awful sick, elderly people out of their misery?'

The other women said nothing. They did not know how to respond. Doing it was one thing. But facing the reality of their actions by talking about it openly outside work seemed too much to contemplate.

Still they were silent. For a moment that same eerie silence that haunted the corridors of the Lainz had returned. It was a significant silence though. For it showed how little these women had even questioned their own killing instincts. They had stifled the life out of all those countless patients – and yet they could not even contemplate talking about it. Waltraud was appalled.

'Come on What do you really think about what we have done? Tell me.'

No response. They really did not know what to say. Here they were being confronted with the facts but they were afraid to speak – much more afraid than they were to kill.

'Let's talk about something else.'

At last, a reaction. Stephanie at least made her feelings clear. She may have helped murder a lot of innocent people but she certainly did not feel it made for good dinner table gossip.

'But we have killed all these people. You must feel something about it? Don't you love the power we have? The influence?'

It was time to change the subject. Waltraud had just discovered that her co-conspirators were nothing more than sheep. Nothing more than Nazi troops doing their duty. They had no feelings.

But someone nearby had heard every word of their conversation – and he was about to try and end their murderous reign of terror.

Dr Franz Pesendorfer was horrified by what he had just heard. Sitting near the group of auxiliary nurses had just revealed one of the biggest mass murders in post-war Europe. The doctor went straight to the police.

Waltraud was a little surprised by the recent changes at Pavilion 5. Some of the newest patients seemed to be rather young – in their 60s and even one in his 50s. This was supposed to be a geriatric ward after all.

She sensed something was not quite right but she just could not be sure what it was. Her basic instincts told her to be careful. She decided the killing had to stop for the time being. It was not as if they were making any money out of the slaughter of the innocent.

It was purely a way to relieve some patients of their agony and get rid of others who had annoyed them by being rude. That was cold blooded murder. No real motive other than the inbuilt sense of power that came with every killing. Anyway, Waltraud decided she should slow down – just in case. Just in case someone had told on her.

The 'younger' patient was indeed an unhappy resident at the Lainz. He hated every second of his stay in that smelly, rotten Pavilion 5 ward. All the nursing staff had quickly grown to dislike him about as much as he loathed them. By a strange twist of fate, if he had been a little older and Waltraud had not been on her guard, then he would definitely have been a candidate for the mouthwash treatment.

In fact, he was a very miserable undercover policeman, planted inside the ward after Dr Pesendorfer had tipped off the Vienna Detectives Bureau following the conversation he had overheard at the beer cellar.

At first the detectives had been scathing about the good doctor's fears. But the hospital administrator had friends in high places so they were forced to respond.

'Old people do tend to die.'

The detective who originally dealt with the case

was just a bit cynical. He could not believe that a few wornen auxiliaries would cold bloodedly murder all these people.

'How can we prove it?'

There was only one way. They would have to be caught in the act.

But Waltraud was on her guard. She knew like all good criminals that something was not right on Pavilion 5 – and she would not risk another kill while the situation prevailed.

Meanwhile, the undercover policeman got more and more depressed. Sleeping in a ward surrounded by dozens of coughing, farting, snoring, groaning old people was not his idea of a plum assignment.

It was hardly surprising when the Vienna Detectives Bureau called off the case following six weeks without so much as a hint of a killing. The good Dr Pesendorfer was stunned that the police were pulling out.

'But you are just allowing them to carry on.'

The policeman was sympathetic to the doctor's plight but he reckoned there were some real criminals out there who needed catching.

Waltraud knew it. She had suspected there was something odd about him from the start. When the news swept around the hospital that an undercover policeman had been a patient on Pavilion 5, it came as no great surprise.

But now he was gone. His tail firmly between his

legs. None the wiser for his awful stay in that depressing ward.

It was time to begin the killing again. She felt the urge. She had earmarked the most likely patients. The ones who had annoyed and insulted her. The pathetic ones who were ready to curl up and die. It was so easy really. The fully trained nurses were never around. They did not care what the auxiliaries did. It had got to the point where no one ever questioned the right of those under-trained assistants to administer drugs and hand out other treatment. That was why Waltraud and her friends had got away with it for so long.

As Waltraud pressed her thumb down on the syringe, she watched the huge dose of insulin rushing into a patient's sickly vein. The elderly women had asked for pain relief so why shouldn't Waltraud give her the ultimate cure – death?

She had grown a little bored of administering the mouthwash. In any case, if there were any spies left on the ward they would be more likely to notice two nurses holding down a patient than the giving of an injection.

'Nurse. Nurse. Has this patient been given any insulin in the past three hours?'

Waltraud looked the young doctor straight in the face.

'No doctor. Not a thing.'

She gave the medic one lingering glance up and down. He is quite a fine looking man, she thought to herself. The welfare of patients was never near the top of Waltraud's list of priorities.

She much preferred to let her mind wander in a world of sexual fantasy. It was so much less depressing. That same elderly women who had been given a huge dose of insulin just an hour before, was close to death – and Waltraud knew it only too well.

Now this rather handsome young doctor was asking awkward questions. How annoying of him, thought Waltraud Wagner. Why doesn't he just let her die? It would seem the sensible course of action.

In any case, in a few more minutes she would be dead – and no one would be any the wiser. Waltraud's mission of murder was on course once more. She had regained the taste for killing after a brief interruption. It was a good feeling. She would have to try to step up the rate. She found herself needing a fix more and more often.

The doctor, however, had other plans for Waltraud. He was very unhappy about that elderly woman's death. He suspected she had been administered an illicit dose of insulin.

Waltraud presumed he was just a fussy medic trying to cover his own inefficiencies.

'They know. They are on to us.'

Waltraud dismissed the alarm bells ringing in her colleagues' voices when they cornered her a few hours later.

'Don't worry. That doctor thinks he will be accused of not looking after his patient properly.'

Though the other women were not convinced,

they had no choice but to accept what Waltraud told them. She held the key to their fate.

Meanwhile the good Dr Pesendorfer had got involved once more. He had never dropped his initial suspicions about the women. Now he was hoping that this new case might be just the breakthrough he had been hoping for.

'I know they have murdered a lot of patients. We cannot let this continue. We must stop them.'

They were the same words he had first uttered two months earlier after overhearing their beer cellar chat. But this time he felt certain they would be brought to justice. He hated the very notion of knowing that four women who had murdered tens if not hundreds of patients still had the free run of the hospital. It was a scandalous situation he was determined to end.

When the autopsy on the elderly woman revealed her body to be riddled with insulin the police were called back into the Lainz General Hospital and Waltraud Wagner and her three accomplices were arrested.

Wagner, Leidolf, Mayen and Gruber were jailed for their roles in the murder and attempted murder of 42 patients at Lainz following their trial in Vienna in March, 1991.

Wagner collapsed in court as she was jailed for life. She had confessed to 10 killings, been found guilty of 15 cases of murder, 17 cases of attempted murder and two cases of inflicting bodily harm.

Leidolf was also given life for five cases of murder

and two cases of attempted murder.

Mayen was jailed for 20 years for a case of manslaughter and seven cases of attempted murder. She too collapsed in the dock and had to be taken out on a stretcher.

Gruber was sentenced to 15 years for two cases of attempted murder.

Wagner had claimed during the trial that she was 'relieving the pain of patients'.

The Judge told her: 'These patients were gasping for breath for up to half a day before they died. You cannot call that pain relief.'

Wagner did not reply.

The Final Cut

Her hair was thick, lustrous and so dark it might have been spun on the same loom as the night. Her shoulders and back were slender. The legs were just as perfect. Jaime Macias could not take his eyes off her, even though he was sitting next to his rather plump wife Aurelia at the time.

He took another swig of his beer and wondered what she would be like in bed. Aurelia studied the expression on her husband's face and knew exactly what he was thinking. She had become well used to his wanderlust, as well as to his violent attacks on her.

Having been married to Jaime Macias for almost twenty years, Aurelia had quietly accepted the suffering because she believed in the sanctity of marriage and the importance of staying together to give the children a stable upbringing. The couple's three children – aged six months to sixteen years – looked on Aurelia as the backbone of the family. Jaime's tendency to drink and disappear for long periods had become an accepted part of life inside the Macias household.

On that particular night – 20 September 1992 – Jaime and Aurelia were attending a christening party for one of her sister's babies in an apartment just a short distance from their home in central Los Angeles, California. Even though it was a relatively formal occasion, Jaime could not behave himself.

Earlier in the evening, he knocked back some extra-strong Mexican tequila before moving back on to beers which he was consuming at an alarming rate. Aurelia was annoyed with her husband for drinking so excessively. Not only was it embarrassing in front of all her relatives, but she knew that the moment they got home she would have submit to his brutal sexual demands.

Watching Jaime lusting after the attractive brunette who was dancing with a younger man particularly enraged Aurelia. She could just about cope with her husband's demands at the best of times, but to be sitting there with him while he fantasised about another woman was, she felt, incredibly insulting.

Naturally, Jaime was completely oblivious to his wife's irritated state of mind. He never once even bothered to look in her direction to see if she had noticed his obsession with the young girl.

'I'm gonna get another beer,' muttered Jaime as he got up. There was no question of asking his 33-year-old wife if she was tired and wanted to go home. He was simply stating a fact to which he did not expect any response.

As Jaime wandered off in the direction of the kitchen, the girl on the dance floor gave him a brief glance. She had felt his eyes upon her as she danced with the other man and she wanted to see what her admirer looked like. At first glance, Jaime Macias, aged 36, was quite a presentable looking Latin type. In fact, it was his swarthy good looks which had first attracted Aurelia to him almost twenty years earlier.

There was no doubting the fact that Jaime noticed the girl looking in his direction because he smiled and raised his eyebrows as he passed by her. Seconds later, she broke off with her dancing partner and slipped into the kitchen.

Throughout this exchange Aurelia was watching everything. She saw the girl glance at her husband. She watched him smile back at her. She even noticed her go into the kitchen after her husband. Unfortunately, it all reminded her of how Jaime had first met her when they were teenagers back in Mexico in the early 1970s.

Aurelia considered getting up and following her husband into the kitchen but she genuinely feared that she would be humiliated if she tried to interrupt him and his new friend. In any case, there wasn't much they could do in the kitchen.

A few minutes later, Jaime emerged with a beer in one hand and the hand of the young girl in the other and they swept past assorted relatives and friends and headed straight for the dance floor. Aurelia turned her face away in disgust. She felt the tendons in her fingers stiffen with tension. How dare he do this in front of her? How dare he call himself her husband?

She started to ask herself why she put up with his behaviour. After all these years of physical, mental and – in her eyes – sexual abuse, he was still prepared to belittle her in front of their closest associates. Why did she put up with it?

Aurelia knew that as many people were watching her response to her husband's blatant behaviour as were looking at him smooching on the dance floor. The women were infuriated. They all shared with Aurelia that same feeling of outrage. They looked in sympathy towards Aurelia. She had tears of anger and bitterness welling up in her eyes. Not once did Jaime even look in her direction. He simply did not care. Neither, it seemed, did the other smiling macho males who kept casting admiring glances in the direction of Jaime and his dancing partner.

That night something made Aurelia even more upset than usual. She started to think that it must have been the way her husband was flouting his adulterous nature right in front of her face. Usually, when he came stumbling home in the early hours stinking of cheap perfume, she could just turn her back on him in bed and ignore the obvious implications of what he had been doing.

This time it was different. She clenched her fists in tight balls of fury and got up to talk to one of her cousins, trying desperately to ignore everything that was happening around her. However, as she talked to the other woman, it became clear that she could not concentrate on what was being said. Her mind was completely focused on just one thing – a rapidly rising hatred for her husband.

She started to wonder if he would commit the ultimate insult and take this girl off somewhere intimate even though his own wife – the mother of his children – was present. Surely he would not be so blatant? She could not be sure. She suspected he had done it in the past.

By now Jaime and his new friend were dancing virtually cheek-to-cheek on the dance floor and other couples were watching and murmuring in each other's ears. Aurelia knew full well what they would be saying.

Suddenly, something inside her snapped. She marched straight up to Jaime and dragged him off the dance floor by his wrist. The men sniggered. The women looked on admiringly.

'Home! Now!' screamed Aurelia, surprised at her

courage in standing up to her husband. At first Jaime looked astounded by his wife's attitude. How dare she talk to him like that – a mere woman whose place was in the home looking after their children. She had no right to tell him to go home.

Aurelia knew what was coming next.

Jaime grabbed her by the wrist and told her in no uncertain terms that he would stay at the party as long as he liked. But Aurelia's fury was still simmering and she reckoned she had nothing to lose.

'What? So you can dance with that woman?'

It was the ultimate insult to a Latino's machismo – his own wife was giving him orders. For a second he considered beating her, but then realised that it would not look good in front of an audience. Instead, Jaime held on to his wife's wrist and marched her straight out of the apartment. No one had the courage to intervene.

As the couple made their way past the rundown apartment block and clipwood, single-storey houses en route to their own home, Jaime shouted fiercely at his wife for daring to insult and embarrass him in front of family and friends. Never once did he apologise for smooching with another woman in front of her very eyes.

'How dare you talk to your husband in such a way! I ought to teach you a lesson,' shouted Jaime.

But Aurelia – who had for so long acted as a human punchbag for her husband – was not going to give in that easily.

'Teach me a lesson? You are lucky I'm still here.

You don't deserve anyone.'

Aurelia fully realised by this time that the only way to avoid the inevitable beating followed by cursory sexual intercourse with her brute of a husband was to counter him on every point. Jaime was too drunk and stupid to take stock of the situation. He failed to recognise the underlying tone of his wife's voice.

By the time they finally arrived back at their cramped apartment, Aurelia had told her husband a few home truths. Strangely, she found herself becoming more and more confident. For the first time in her married life she felt as if she was actually taking the upper hand.

As Jaime began partially to sober up he should have started to take some notice but the moment they got into the flat he poured himself a huge tequila – and that was when Aurelia realised things were about to go from bad to worse.

She knew her husband was not drunk enough simply to collapse on top of the bed as he had done frequently in the past. That tequila would simply fuel his animal instincts and that would mean the nearest thing to matrimonial rape for Aurelia.

The moment they got into the bedroom, their youngest child, Jorge, started crying. Aurelia had never been so relieved to hear a child cry in her life. She believed that it would signal the end of her husband's clumsy efforts at making love.

As was often the case with Jorge, the child needed feeding so Aurelia did the thing that comes most naturally to mothers. She exposed her bosom and lay down on the bed to try to get their youngest child to sleep. Jaime had other ideas.

Within seconds of starting to breast-feed the child, Aurelia became aware that her husband was far from asleep. He was lying watching her and then he tried to fondle her. Aurelia was appalled.

'Get your hands off me, you animal!'

Momentarily Jaime stopped trying to touch his wife's breasts. Then he started running his hand further down her body. This time the tension inside Aurelia positively exploded.

'Get away from me! Get away from me!'

Jaime could not see there was any problem.

'Just do as I want, you whore!'

'You left the whore back at that party!'

Aurelia was all set to leave the matrimonial bed but then she heard Jaime snoring loudly within seconds of his last remark. Finally, the demon drink had got the better of him.

She finished feeding little Jorge and put him back in his crib. However, Aurelia was far from ready for bed. Her husband's behaviour that night had driven her to the edge of despair. She really wondered if it was worth the misery and depravity to keep their marriage intact.

As Aurelia lay next to her smelly, snoring husband she found her mind abuzz with fear and loathing. She was feeling more incensed and angry than ever before. The attempt at sex in front of their infant son was simply the final straw. She started to think about getting revenge on him for all those years of brutality and infidelity.

Her mind kept flashing back to earlier that evening when he was dancing with the other woman. She knew then and there that he must have had dozens of women since they got married. She had ignored everything up until now but now she felt an urge to get even, to make him pay for the suffering he had caused.

Aurelia slipped quietly out of bed and moved gently across the room to the tiny kitchen off the main hallway of the apartment. Her hands were not shaking, she was not in tears, she was just coldly determined. She had made up her mind.

She slid open the drawer in the kitchen cabinet and looked down at the contents. A pair of gardening shears glistened in the light pouring in from a street lamp outside the kitchen window.

Aurelia grasped the handles of the shears, lifted them out silently and walked back to the bedroom.

On the bed lay the ever-snoring heap of a human being who was her husband, her brutal, adulterous, wife-beating husband. She kept seeing rapid images of all the things he had done to her flash before her eyes.

It was blisteringly hot as evening temperatures in Los Angeles were hitting ninety degrees, so Jaime was wearing only his pyjama bottoms. He had a sheet partly covering his waist but little else.

Still grasping the garden shears, Aurelia looked down at him. She carefully opened the gap at the front of the pyjamas so that she could just make out the sight of his flaccid penis and hairy scrotum. She knelt gently and quietly on the bed next to her husband and tried to place the shears around the base of his limp member. However, they would not open wide enough, even though his member was so small and shrivelled up. She realised that it would be virtually impossible to cut it clean off in one swift movement. She paused to reconsider her plan of attack.

Just then, Jaime moved right on to his back in his sleep. It was a considerate move on his part for it exposed his entire genital area to Aurelia. She looked down and realised that Jaime's scrotum was actually more clearly defined than his penis, which had shrunken to such a small size.

For a moment, Aurelia tried to snap herself out of her mission to destroy her husband's manhood. Then she reminded herself of all the abuse he had inflicted on her with that thing – and thought about all the other women he had serviced with it as well. This time she was going to make him pay.

Jaime Macias awoke at exactly 4am with an incredible pain in his groin. Still inebriated from his mammoth drinking bout earlier, he fell out of bed and struggled in the direction of the bathroom. Switching on the light he looked down to see his pyjama bottoms soaked in blood. Then he dropped them to the floor and realised that his testicles had been completely severed.

Jaime remembers nothing else after that because he

collapsed with shock at that moment. His eldest son rushed into the bathroom and immediately called the police. All the time, Aurelia looked on without making any attempt to help her husband. The look of blank satisfaction said it all. She had got her revenge ...

The Macias separated after the attack and Aurelia was charged with corporal injury to a spouse, a felony which carries a maximum four-year prison term. Further charges of mayhem were made by LA's deputy district attorney Larry Longo after he learned of the serious nature of the injuries to Jaime Macias.

In March 1994, however, Aurelia was acquitted of the main charges against her and the jury were unable to reach a verdict on a lesser charge of battery.

Jury forewoman Claudia Marshall told the judge that Aurelia Macias had been 'verbally and emotionally abused throughout the marriage' but she denied that the jury had been swayed by the fact that Jaime wanted to drop the charges against his wife.

Aurelia's defence lawyer insisted her client should never have been brought to trial and the couple are now reconciled, with Jaime promising to mend his ways.

Footnote: Only one of Jaime Macias's testicles was recovered, and not until the day after the attack, so doctors were unable to reattach it.

Under the Willow Tree

'What's this shit?'

Tom Scotland had a way with words which few people appreciated, least of all his good wife June. His favourite response at meal times was to throw the remains of his food right at her if it did not meet his approval.

And on that particular day in the summer of 1987, he was keeping to his own traditional behaviour pattern yet again. This time it was the meat pie that induced the Tom Scotland pig-of-the-month performance.

'Call this food? A leper wouldn't touch it, you useless piece of shit.'

Twenty years. She'd put up with it since the beginning. Sometimes she wondered why. But then she remembered the kids. Someone had to look after them, bring them up in the world and teach them the basics. And Tom Scotland wasn't much of a father, so it was all left to June.

As she removed the bits of pie crust and splodgy gravy from her housecoat, she really did wonder if it was all worth it. She looked down at him sitting smugly there at the dinner table stamping his feet, and let the loathing build up.

How dare he treat her like that? What right had he to shout and abuse her? Other women would have left long ago. Even her relatives had tried to persuade her. Just walk out on him. But for the children ... She had to protect them. She had no job, no independent income. June Scotland was trapped, but she was finally coming to the conclusion that it was time to start planning her escape.

As she stood there in the kitchen of their modest three-bedroomed house in Stevenage, she felt a new, hardened anger flood through her. But June was quickly snapped out of those thoughts when Scotland came charging towards the fridge.

Before she could utter a word, he ripped it open and started grappling through the contents like some desperate beggar on the streets of Calcutta. Soon the contents were spread all over the kitchen floor and her husband was cursing them just as much as he cursed June at the dinner table.

'What's this?' He threw a dish of stew she had lovingly prepared into the air. The brown gravy splattered across the floor she had spent so much time making pristinely clean just a few hours earlier.

'And this?' He pulled out a plate load of uncooked hamburgers and ground them into the cracks between the tiles with the heel of his work boots.

'Why can't you ever make me the sort of food I like? Not this rubbish.'

June was heartbroken. It had happened before. But this time it was really hitting her hard. She wondered how she had managed to endure all those years of insults. He had no right treating her this way. But what could she do? In reality, there was only one answer. That day marked the start of the countdown to Tom Scotland's death.

'But do they work?'

June Scotland was most concerned about whether the travel sickness tablets she was about to purchase at her local chemist really were effective.

When she asked about obvious precautions like not taking them together with sleeping pills, the shop assistant must have thought she was a pretty sensible lady simply preparing for a holiday in some sunshine location. For the residents of Stevenage, Spain was probably the most popular place to go, although June had no intention of even getting on an aeroplane, let alone spending any time away from her tidy little house in Pankhurst Crescent.

As she walked back home through the quiet, neat streets, she could feel a real buzz of excitement from within. It was almost as if she were going on a holiday. She was so looking forward to this time next week. She would be free for the first time in 22 years. No more emotional torture. No more pain and suffering. No more sleepless nights filled with the fear of what tomorrow holds. But, most important of all, there would be no more opportunities for that animal to get his hands on their daughter.

That was what hurt June the most. Less than four years earlier her pretty dark-haired daughter had come home from school one day looking like death. Her face was pale. Her eyes were watery. She was shaking with fear. Caroline Scotland was just 15 years old and the truth had just dawned on her that her father – her own flesh and blood, the man who had helped bring her into the world – had been forcing her to have sex with him.

At first, he'd touched her and stroked her in places that did not seem natural. That was when she was just 11 years old. He would catch her in the garden and carry her into the shed, where he would sit her down and start to let his fingers run lines across her soft, young skin. She did not even realise what he was doing at first. Something told her that it was not right. But she was afraid to tell anyone, even her mum. It seemed better just to let things be. She did not want to start yet another fight between her parents. She had seen enough of the rows to last a lifetime. She did not want to be the cause of more.

But then it got more serious. Scotland was not content with gratifying his sick sexual demands through touching and feeling. He wanted more. By the time Caroline had reached her teens she was no longer a virgin. Her innocence had been bruised and destroyed by that animal who called himself her father. For two years, he carried on thrusting his perverted demands on his daughter. He preyed on her innermost fears. He threatened her with awful consequences if she so much as mentioned a word of it to her mother.

Basically, she was suppressing the truth from herself, as is often the case with victims of incest. He would do the act. She would go back to sleep. The next day, those dreadful memories would be locked out of her mind, hidden away in a fragment of her brain that would keep them safe until something sparked them off again.

For at least two years that part of her mind absorbed the sexual abuse and then tucked it away out of sight. It was only when she began talking with her friends at school about sex that she realised with a shocking force that what he did to her was completely and utterly wrong. And the picture came back together ...

At first, they were just quick flashes. A hand on her knee. Her dress buttons being unfastened. The flare of his hairy nostrils as he leaned close to her lips. After that, the dam burst and she relived the experiences with sickening clarity. Finally, she could take no more and decided to tell her mum.

Like any caring mother, June was horrified. The man she had once loved and cherished had forced their innocent little daughter to have sex with him. The two of them just wept in each other's arms.

Caroline tried to take her own life. It was June's most terrifying experience. Walking in on her as she was in the process of attempting to kill herself. Luckily, June prevented the tragedy, but she could do nothing to stop Caroline's nightmares. Like the time her father took her favourite teddy bear and threw it in the blazing fireplace just because she had written on the wall. He did not spare his two sons either. They nicknamed him 'Mr Killjoy'. But it turned out to be a tragic underestimate of his real intentions towards his family.

The two days following her purchase of those travel sickness pills were filled with anguish for June Scotland.

The plan to end her marriage to a monster was underway, but she wondered if she really would have the courage to see it through. She kept playing with that tiny bottle of tablets in her handbag every time she thought about what to do. But she simply could not get herself to take them out and make the inevitable happen.

Each night, when he came home from his job as an electrician, she found herself thrown back into his awful, abusive world. The insults were continuous. It was like the worst kind of mental torture and, yet, what made it even more painful was the knowledge that she now had the power to end his life. All she had to do was unscrew that bottle and pour the pills into his food. It was that easy.

But it wasn't until the third morning – on 25 August, 1987 – that June made the fateful decision that would alter the course of her entire life.

As usual, she woke up early to prepare the breakfast that her bullying husband always expected. She turned to face him in the bed. When he actually slept, it was the only time he looked vaguely pleasant. But beneath those closed eyelids, she knew the monster was still very much alive – and in just a few minutes the inevitable torture would begin all over again.

June Scotland had decided. She lay there in the bed next to him and thought: 'Yes, today is the day I'm going to kill you.' That was it. She had promised herself it would happen. Not just for her. For the sake of Caroline. For the sake of a peaceful, happy life.

'Hey! What's all this? We celebratin' something?'

Even when his wife prepared his favourite meal of stir-fry turkey, Tom Scotland could not sound in the least bit grateful. Most husbands would have grabbed their wife and kissed her in recognition of the special effort. But not Scotland. It was almost as if he preferred coming home to pour scorn and abuse on his family. Happiness did not come easily to Tom Scotland.

He eyed his wife suspiciously across the kitchen. His instincts told him she was up to something. When June turned and faced him, she knew she was doing the right thing. Maybe if he had shown some compassion or loving towards her, then she might have felt a twinge of guilt and perhaps she would have decided to abandon her plan.

But, instead, he was playing right into her hands. His gruff, ungrateful manner was yet more confirmation in her own mind that he was about to get what he deserved.

As usual, the meal was eaten in virtual silence. Caroline was upstairs listening to records in her room. She preferred not to eat in the presence of her father. She could not stand to feel his eyes bearing down on her from the sofa, where he sat glued to the television as he ate. She could not handle the knowledge that he was sitting there having devoured her body in every sense. The very thought that he was so close to her in front of her mother filled Caroline with disgust and loathing. She preferred to be alone with her thoughts. Why should she exchange pleasantries with that animal?

June Scotland sat down opposite her husband in the lounge and watched him eating the stir-fry turkey with a feeling of immense satisfaction. At last the time had come. She examined each mouthful as he scoffed back the food. She thought she could see the white remnants of those forty-odd travel sickness pills in amongst the turkey and vegetables. She hesitated for a moment when he caught her staring straight at his plate. But he said nothing. Tom Scotland had long since given up communicating with his wife. He was not about to change the habit of a lifetime by questioning her actions now.

Any normal, loving husband might have at least complimented June on her culinary skills. Not this husband though. He just carried on pitch-forking the food into his mouth. June watched him and smiled inside. He attacked the dinner as though it were his last ...

June was already starting to feel that sense of relief that comes after you have achieved something you so carefully set out to do. She retreated to the kitchen because she could not stand to watch him any longer. Her emotions were torn in two. Here she was, killing the man she had promised to love and adore for the rest of her life. Yet every time she looked at him she knew why it just had to be done.

She peered through the kitchen hatch. He mopped his plate with a piece of bread and let out a contented burp. For once, such a sweet sound. It was a signal. It would not be long now ...

Tom Scotland was not feeling at all well. Within minutes of finishing that last mouthful of his favourite meal, he tried to get up to go to the toilet and almost fell flat on his face. He closed his eyes for a moment. The image of that food was swimming around inside his head. It made him feel nauseous, so he blinked open his eyes once more. The room was moving. He could hardly focus on his beloved TV set, let alone make out what show was on.

He tried again to get to his feet. This time he just made it by holding onto the arm of the sofa, but it was a real struggle. One step at a time, he tried to move toward the door. He nearly fell over a chair and just regained his balance.

By the time Tom Scotland got to the hallway from the living room, he felt as if he'd just walked a hundred miles. From the kitchen, June watched him without uttering a word. One half of her felt like helping him but the other, more realistic half, stopped her. She could not, and would not, save him. This was all meant to be.

Heavy rock music blared out from his daughter's room. He wished she would turn the bloody thing off, but he hadn't the strength to shout. When Tom Scotland caught a glimpse of his wife watching him calmly from the kitchen, it dawned on him for the first time that she had just sentenced him to death. Even through his swirling thoughts, he could see it in her eyes. This time, it was her turn to show no emotion. Her hands were folded tersely in front of her. He knew.

'Get the doctor.'

He could barely utter the words. And when he did, it felt as if someone else was saying them. But June did not move towards him as he half collapsed there on the floor. She did not say a word as he crawled, like some wounded soldier, slowly up the stairs towards his bedroom.

Instead, she quietly pulled open the nearest drawer in the kitchen and took out a rolling pin. The very object that is so often used to illustrate a wife's anger with her husband was now about to become the ultimate weapon.

By the time she got to the stairs, he had already managed to crawl through the bedroom door. She knew she had to be quick, otherwise he might get to the telephone.

The first blow of that rolling pin smashed into the side of his head as he crawled towards the sanctuary of his bed. Incredibly, it helped rather than hindered Scotland's fight for life. Somehow, the blow to his head helped clear his mind momentarily. His vision straightened out significantly and any doubts about his wife's intentions had been wiped from his mind.

He grabbed hold of the rolling pin and tried to yank it out of his wife's grasp. They grappled like two sumo wrestlers on the floor of the bedroom. She managed to hold onto her weapon of destruction though.

Then Tom Scotland tried to make for the door as another blow rained past his head, missing him by inches. It was his only chance. He had to get out of that room.

The heavy rock music was still blaring out from Caroline's room, drowning out the sound of the deadly attack that was about to reach a crescendo.

But June was not going to let him get away. She pursued him onto the landing outside the bedrooms. It was a small floorspace and, as the husband and wife continued their life-and-death struggle, they fell down the stairs. Rolling like stuntmen out of a cops-and-robbers film, they seemed to keep falling in slow motion as the angle of the stairway slowed their descent.

June was the first one to get up when they landed at the foot of the stairs. She still had that rolling pin grasped in her hand. A look of steely determination on her face. For a moment she looked down at the pathetic mess of a man who had once claimed he loved her. Then he stirred and tried to get back on his feet. By moving, he simply encouraged the killer instinct within June to rear up again. To finish off the job she had set out to do.

The last blow went crashing through his skull with all the strength she could summon. The blood from the wound splattered everywhere in the hallway as the noise of Caroline's heavy metal record reached its own musical crescendo at exactly the same moment. Bits of gristle splattered the floor and walls. That last crunching blow literally crushed his brain to bits.

June stood there for a moment taking in the scene. It all seemed so unreal. Had she really just done all that to her husband? For a few minutes she could not absorb the reality of the situation. It was as if she were completely detached from it. Only when her daughter Caroline appeared beside her did it really all dawn on her.

Caroline was 18 years old, but those memories of her father's illicit sexual intercourse with her were as fresh as yesterday in her mind. That's why she showed no emotion as she looked down at his twisted, pathetic body lying there in a crumpled heap on the floor.

With her mother standing beside her, she stared into his matt, glazed eyes. There was no flicker of life left in them. Nothing. But still they had a strange hypnotic effect on her. It was as if the devil inside him was waiting to leap out at her and drag her into the bedroom for yet more sexual abuse.

She checked for pulses in the neck and wrist – there was nothing. Her mother watched her admiringly. Amazed that her little baby could be so professional. So calm. So cool. So collected. But there were other thoughts running through Caroline's mind. She could not keep her eyes off him. Her gaze kept being drawn to his face. The mask of death.

'Even when he was dead he looked evil,' said Caroline later.

She leant down and closed his eyelids firmly. It was a remarkable attempt to seek reassurance that the monster had finally departed from that terrified household.

'It was like she hadn't killed him, that he was alive. He looked evil and I had to shut them.'

Mother and daughter exchanged few words. The shock of witnessing the end of their torment spoke louder than any words. Caroline decided she had to take control of the situation. Her mother was shaking with fear. She had done it, but now she was terrified of the consequences. Her teenage daughter – always incredibly close to June – was about to show maturity well beyond her age. She was going to grow up right before her mother's very eyes.

The bottle of Bacardi was shaking as June Scotland poured it into two tumblers for her and her daughter. They sat on the same sofa where only a few minutes earlier Tom Scotland had devoured that poisoned feast which marked the start of his journey to death.

The door to the living room was shut. They did not want to be able to see the bloody remains of Tom Scotland as they discussed what to do next. There was little doubt in Caroline's mind – she was not going to let the man who abused and terrorised her drag them both into the arms of the law. She was convinced that there was a way to avoid all that.

Two stiff Bacardis later they had agreed a plan. June's oldest son Alan had long since moved out of home and her other son Alistair was away. The house was empty except for the two of them. They had time on their side.

Caroline dropped a sheet over the bloody remains of her father so that it covered him from head to toe. No hint of his bluing, pallid skin was exposed. The last thing either of them wanted was to have to see him there whenever they walked through the hallway.

June was about to go into her bedroom – the same room she had shared with the monster – when she remembered the bloody evidence of her first crushing blow to his head was spread around the carpet. It was too much. She could not bear to go in there. She stopped Caroline on the landing and persuaded her to sleep with her in young Alistair's room. It was the only place in that tiny, modest house where there were no actual reminders of the killing that had just occurred.

Neither June nor Caroline had a particularly good night's sleep. Their waking moments were filled with the living nightmare they had just endured. Their dreams were filled with even more graphic, outrageous images brought on by the real-life horrors they had just been involved in.

The early dawn light had only just started peeping through the curtains in Alistair's bedroom when the two women decided they had to get up to complete their grisly task.

'Come on. Let's just get on with it.'

Caroline was now firmly in charge. She was paying him back for all that abuse. She could not stand the thought of her mother paying the penalty for something she wished she'd done herself.

Armed with mops, clothes, rubber gloves and every cleaning implement they could find, the two women began methodically cleaning the house from top to bottom. Spring-cleaning time had come early in the Scotland household.

After hours of fanatical scrubbing, Caroline and June laid their mops on the floor for a moment and looked down from the landing at the crumpled sheet that covered what was once the brutal, bruising figure of 48-year-old Tom Scotland. They still had not touched the body. It was as if they were subconsciously hoping that by cleaning the house, his body might just magically disappear and they would not have to face the gruesome task of disposing of the corpse.

But he was still there when Caroline clinically lifted the sheet to start the operation to dispose of his body.

They struggled to wrap the body in a plastic sheet. Every time they managed to lift up one end of his stiff, lifeless body they couldn't quite squeeze it under. Finally, after many attempts, they managed to seal Tom Scotland from the outside world for ever.

His body looked weirdly distorted through the plastic covering. Luckily, it gave the whole proceedings an unreal aura. His skin had changed colour and he no longer looked like the evil man both women had grown to hate.

'Let's take him to the shed.'

Caroline was once again firmly in charge. She lifted him from the heavier end as her mum struggled to hold his legs. Caroline was thankful that she had closed his eyelids the previous night. The very thought of him staring coldly at her through the plastic, as they half dragged him through the pitch black that next evening, would have probably scared her to death.

As it was, both women had somehow mentally detached themselves from the task at hand – and things were by no means over yet.

After dumping his rotting corpse on the muddy floor of the garden shed, Caroline looked around herself for a moment and remembered those horrific times just a few years earlier when he would take her in that very same shed and touch her and hurt her.

It must have given her the strangest feeling of satisfaction to know that she had voluntarily walked back into that shed now – with his lifeless body completely under her control this time. There was absolutely nothing he could do to prevent her from getting revenge for all those appalling attacks.

It wasn't until the following evening that June and Caroline finally got rid of him. Once again, it was the daughter who came to the rescue.

As June sat shaking with nerves in the kitchen, Caroline grabbed hold of her father's favourite spade and started digging his grave for him.

It took four hours to get the hole big enough. Caroline was completely exhausted. She had no idea it would be so difficult when she set out to dig the grave. It wasn't helped by the fact that she had to do it all in complete silence for fear that one of the nosy neighbours of Pankhurst Crescent might hear something suspicious and call the police.

But at least she had picked a spot just beneath his favourite (and only) weeping willow tree. He did not deserve any sympathy, but it seemed only right to lie him to rest amongst the rotting roots of that vast tree which had dominated Caroline's view from her bedroom window for most of her life.

Back in the kitchen, June was nervously sipping at her favourite drink, Bacardi. She was dreading the next stage in their plan – the lowering of the body. She kept having nightmarish thoughts about him still being alive. Breaking free of that plastic covering and killing them all in an act of bitter-sweet revenge. She really did not want to go out there on that warm August night and even so much as see the shape of his corpse through the plastic.

'Come on, mum. The quicker we do it, the better.' Caroline was almost business-like about it all, but she was merely stifling her emotions so as not to make things any worse for her mother. That was her priority all along – her mum. Yet, she herself had a lot to gain by getting rid of him for ever. Her life might actually start to be worth living again. Perhaps those – suicidal feelings would go away for ever. It was worth getting rid of him for that alone.

'I can't go through with this – I want to end it now and tell someone.'

June had broken down in tears. The prospect of burying her own husband was too much. Caroline had to think quick. This was not the way it was meant to be.

'No one will understand why you did it. We've got to do it this way.'

June took another almighty swig of Bacardi, held her head up high and walked single-mindedly out to the end of the garden, just beneath the weeping willow.

The thud that sounded as his body crashed into the shallow grave just beneath the weeping willow tree was muted. It did not echo.

'I'm sorry.'

Caroline looked in astonishment at her mother. She was apologising to the monster who had so nearly ruined all their lives.

The sound of the earth being sprinkled over the plastic sheeting was quite distinct at first. Each shovel load landed with a definite noise.

'I'm sorry.'

She said those words again. Caroline tried to understand why her mother should feel any sorrow for that man, but she could not truly appreciate it.

It was only after his entire body had been completely covered by its first layer of earth that the noise became more muffled and insignificant. It was also then that June Scotland stopped saying sorry to her husband.

'He's gone to work in Saudi Arabia. Won't be back for years.'

It seemed the perfect excuse for Tom Scotland's absence. Some concerned neighbours replied: 'That's a long time. Won't you miss him?' But June Scotland ignored those remarks and just got on with her life.

For three and a half years no one questioned her or her family about his departure. It was as if most people were glad to see the back of him; otherwise, perhaps they would have cared a little more.

June was just relieved to have a life to live once more. She loved staying at home and looking after the baby Caroline had had a year or so after her father's death. Often they'd both sit at the kitchen table and look out at that stretch of grass at the end of the garden and think about him. But it was always merely a passing thought. There was no regret. They knew it had had to be done. They shared the ultimate secret but they never once felt tempted to tell anyone else. Their mother–daughter relationship was strangely bonded even more closely by the events that had occurred. It was as if they were both just grateful for the chance to live again.

Neither Caroline nor June seemed unduly worried when their houseproud neighbour Ted Bunce decided to erect a new, pristine garden fence just near the weeping willow.

As Ted dug a series of small holes in the ground to make the fence more stable, he could not possibly have known what lay just under his feet - until he spotted the plastic sheet coming through the soil. And through that cover he noticed a hand. He stopped digging immediately.

June Scotland felt numb as she looked through her living room window to see police cordoning off the back garden. Suddenly the full realisation of what had happened three and half years earlier dawned on her. She knew full well why they were there. In her heart of hearts she had known this day would eventually come, despite her daughter's sterling efforts to cover up the death of Tom Scotland.

With tears streaming down her face, she ran through the house. But this was no desperate attempt to escape. She knew she had to do one thing before they called at her door and arrested her.

She knocked desperately on the door of her son Alistair's room. He was stunned when she said to him: 'I've got something to tell you.'

'Is it granny or grandad?' asked Alistair, sensing the impending doom in her voice.

'No. Worse. They've found your father in the garden. I hit him with a rolling pin.'

Alistair hugged his mother tightly and they just stood there for a few seconds in silence. Then there was a knock at the door.

June Scotland took a deep breath, went downstairs and calmly let the police in.

In March 1992, June Scotland, aged 52, was sentenced to two years' probation after being convicted at Luton Crown Court of manslaughter on the grounds of diminished responsibility. A jury cleared her of the greater charge of murder after Judge Justice Garland said:

'No good whatsoever would be served by seeking to punish you further.'

Her daughter Caroline received two years' probation after admitting preventing a lawful burial. Justice Garland told her:

'When you were 18 you found yourself in a situation that must have been impossible, almost an intolerable burden on you.'

June Scotland has now changed her surname by deed poll after announcing: 'The name of Scotland is too unusual. We plan to move somewhere and start a new life.'

Tragically, she is estranged from both her sons following her arrest for the murder of their father.

The Only Answer

When 11-year-old Karen Bigham heard her 12-year-old brother Paul let out another cry, she trembled with fear, too scared to say anything as she lay in her bed. She hoped and prayed that the beating had finished, that their bullying stepfather had ended his violent tirade against the boy.

Karen looked across as Paul came into the room weeping and snivelling following the attack he had suffered at the hands of vicious, twisted Archie

Bigham, and wondered how it had all ended so cruelly for them.

Only a few years earlier, in 1979, the brother and sister had been delighted when Archie formally adopted them after marrying their mother Terri. It meant they had a father again. By 1987, however, Archie and Terri had split up and a tragedy was about to unfold.

The first piece of bad luck occurred when there was a fire at the house Karen and Paul shared with their mother in the Essex seaside town of Southend. The property was gutted and while Terri looked for another home, the children had to move into their adopted father's house in nearby Barking.

At first things had been all right, but then Archie Bigham had started beating young Paul. That was just the beginning.

Not content with inflicting terror on Paul, Archie also turned his attentions towards little Karen. Too scared to do or say anything, she was forced to take part in sick and perverted sexual acts which effectively stole her childhood from her.

The confused schoolgirl could not understand why he was doing these dreadful things. Her confidence was gradually shattered by the relentless nature of his molestations. The man she had admired for so long was betraying her trust and hurting her both physically and mentally.

Every time Bigham entered a room in that house, Karen feared he was about to inflict more pain and suffering. The abuse went on for many months and Karen began to withdraw into herself more and more, all the time building up a reservoir of hatred and resentment for that evil man who still insisted on calling himself her father.

At one stage she began to wonder if it was all her fault. Maybe she had invited his perverted lust? Perhaps she had caused it all? All the classic feelings of guilt began to dominate her thoughts. The worst aspect of all was that the fear and shame had combined to persuade Karen not to reveal the horrific attacks to anyone. Such is the shame suffered by victims of abuse.

At night, Karen would cry herself to sleep. Sometimes she even hoped she would not wake up again the next day. When she did wake, there was an overriding feeling of disappointment that everything had not been just a dreadful nightmare. The reality became harder and harder to cope with.

Karen had few friends at school because she had become so withdrawn. Some teased her because they thought she was timid. If only they had realised what anguish she was going through.

It was not until Karen reached her teens that she even allowed herself the luxury of thinking that perhaps all those attacks had not been her fault after all. It took a tearful admission to her mother Terri to make her realise that he was the monster and that he should be punished for inflicting such harm on an innocent child.

Terri was understandably appalled when she heard from Karen what had happened. She felt a real sense of betrayal by the man who had at one time seemed like the perfect father to her children.

Within hours of hearing Karen's horrific account, Terri visited her local police station and initiated an investigation into the activities of Bigham. Afterwards, she consoled the terrified Karen by assuring her that soon that animal would be locked up where he could not cause her or any other children any harm.

Karen hoped that the cloud of fear would diminish. Maybe for the first time in years, she might feel she could enter into a friendship without worrying that it might end up as an act of betrayal like the ultimate sin that had been committed on her by Bigham.

For any sexually abused child the most difficult aspect is to try to get on with one's life. To try to start to rebuild confidence in other people after such a dreadful crime has been perpetrated. Karen believed that, finally, she might actually have a life to look forward to.

In March 1991, when Karen was fifteen, Archie Bigham finally appeared before a judge at Snaresbrook Crown Court in east London, to face charges. Looking shamefaced after hearing the sordid details of the attacks he had inflicted on his stepdaughter, he pleaded guilty to three charges of indecently assaulting Karen and asked for eleven other offences to be taken into consideration.

Karen was elated. At last she felt that justice had

been done. All those years of never being able to get that monster out of her mind might now be coming to a close. The man who'd scarred her life was about to be locked away for a long time. Or so she thought.

Somehow – even though Bigham had admitted being a repeated child molester – he was sentenced to just three years' probation.

Sitting in the court waiting to see him given what he deserved, Karen was astounded. This was the man who made her do things that no child should ever have to endure. This was the man who felt absolutely no remorse for his perverted habits. This was the man who had ruined her life.

Karen put her head in her hands when it was explained to her that probation meant Bigham would not serve one day in prison. He was free to walk from that court. He was free to come back and haunt her and he was free to molest and abuse other youngsters.

The fact that the court insisted he behave himself for the next three years or face being slung into jail meant nothing to Karen. The fact of the matter was that her stepfather had been simply slapped on the wrists for being a paedophile. Where was the justice in that?

As Karen seethed over the lenient sentence, she felt almost as much hurt as she had during all those long months of sexual torture and abuse. Would the nightmare ever end? Karen promised herself she would resolve the situation somehow, even if it meant having to resort to her own brand of justice.

In July 1991, she devised a plan. She knew the precise movements of her evil stepfather and she was going to make him suffer. As he walked in the street one day, she and a friend ambushed and attacked Bigham. She could see in his eyes that he knew full well why they were after him. He put up no resistance as he was left reeling in the street after two crushing blows to the head.

Karen warned him never to do what he did to her again. Bigham did not reply.

Afterwards, Karen felt a surge of satisfaction at having carried out the attack. She had gained revenge and maybe now he would keep away from all children, although she somehow doubted it.

The irony was that this whole sad story might have ended there if it had not been for Archie Bigham's insatiable appetite for children. He had absolutely no control over his urges and as he got older he seemed to feel the need to attack and molest youngsters with ever-increasing regularity. Secretly, he was plotting an even more outrageous crime than that to which he had subjected poor Karen.

Karen, now sixteen, sat on the comfortable sofa at home and watched as her mother Terri clasped her hands together nervously. She seemed to have something to say but she was having the utmost difficulty getting it out.

As Terri wrestled with the problem of what to say and how to tell her daughter, Karen already had an inkling about what was about to be revealed. She had suffered so much during her short life that she knew the tell-tale signs in her mother's nervousness.

'There's something I should tell you about your stepdad,' whispered Terri.

Before her mother could explain what she meant, Karen had already guessed the awful truth. She felt sick and faint. She knew that he had been committing more horrendous crimes and that he had made other young innocents suffer.

'He's done it again, Karen,' explained Terri. 'Only this time to a four-year-old girl.'

Karen felt completely nauseous now. In her mind she could see him doing those horrible things to her when she was eleven. She pictured it happening when she was four and it was too much to contemplate.

There was an awkward silence between mother and daughter. Karen's mind was still filled with appalling images but that silence was like the calm before the storm.

Terri continued, 'It wasn't just the little girl this time. He's raped the mother as well.'

The shadow of that evil monster falling across her bed at night-time leapt. Into her mind as clearly as if he was there in the room with them. For a few seconds, Karen was an 11-year-old again, the one who'd hidden under the bedcovers whenever she heard her stepfather's footsteps coming up the stairs at night.

The latest perversion starring Archie Bigham seemed to Karen almost like another victory for child molesters. She felt he was saying, 'I'll never be stopped. I'm going to molest as many children as I can get my hands on.'

At that moment Karen decided she would guarantee that he never got away with it again.

It was July and Karen should have been looking forward to life on a sunny summer's day. She'd just passed eight GCSE exams with flying colours and her future seemed bright.

However, there was a cloud hanging over everything and that cloud was Archie Bigham. She could not get him out of her mind. The evil, sick, perverted monster seemed determined to ruin her entire family. He had to be stopped.

Yet again, the police launched a major investigation into the sexual activities of Bigham. They were dealing with a known paedophile, so the officers were hardly surprised by the new allegations.

On 26 August 1991, Bigham was arrested for assault. At the time he'd been attending a course designed to stop sex offenders from striking again. He was released on bail while investigations continued.

Karen was outraged that Bigham should have been released. It seemed like the final injustice to her. The man who had abused and terrorised her and then committed even worse crimes with a mother and a four-year-old was being allowed to walk free yet again. To rub salt into the wounds of her fury, he had been released on bail pending an eventual trial. Nobody seemed prepared to put this monster behind bars.

Karen was a ball of knotted-up tension by this

stage. She was desperate to pour her feelings out to someone and began confiding in a friend, 27-year-old Vince Scott. He had met her at a burger bar on the Southend seafront where she worked in a summer job.

As holidaymakers swarmed in and out of the restaurant, Karen and Vince discussed how to remedy the situation with Bigham. Vince was just as outraged as Karen when she told him the story. After he had heard it all, Karen got down to brass tacks.

'Will you sort it out?'

Vince did not hesitate in his reply. 'I'll do him.'

'I want him done good. It doesn't matter if he ends up in a pine box.'

With those words, Archie Bigham's fate was sealed. Although Karen had never truly intended to murder the pervert. She undoubtedly wanted him to suffer.

Within days, Karen's older brother Paul was also recruited into the team to 'get' Bigham.

The plan was to give the paedophile a good beating and make him suffer the way he made so many others suffer. He was going to get a taste of his own medicine.

On Bank Holiday Monday, 31 August 1992, Bigham went to his local pub. While he was out, Vince and Paul broke into the pervert's home in Barking. Vince handed Paul a knife and they sat and waited for Bigham to return.

The paedophile finally stumbled into the house in the early hours, completely unaware of his visitors. The two men caught him totally by surprise, grabbed him and forced him to sit at a table so that they could begin their interrogation.

'Why do you do it? What sexual satisfaction do you get out of abusing kids?' said Vince, his voice quivering with anger and disgust.

Archie did not reply. He could not, not without incriminating himself further. He just sat in silence, waiting for the next move.

Meanwhile Paul was working himself into a terrible rage. Not only did he keep thinking about the sexual abuse that man had committed on his innocent young sister but he also kept remembering all the physical abuse he had taken from Bigham.

Paul began repeatedly stabbing the wooden table right in front of the convicted pervert. Bigham sweated as he watched.

'I'm going to kill you! I'm going to kill you! I'm going to kill you!'

Bigham looked terrified. He knew he had to say something, otherwise his fate would be sealed. Slowly, he mumbled little titbits of information. The two men made him speak more clearly. It was then that Bigham admitted inflicting all those beatings on Paul. He confessed to sexually abusing Karen and those other relatives. Archie Bigham was battling for his life. He was admitting his most heinous crimes in exchange for survival ... or so he hoped.

However, providing the sordid details of his most recent molestation simply incited his assailants. Vince exploded, grabbed the knife from Paul and stabbed Bigham viciously. Paul got the weapon back from his pal and followed suit almost immediately. They were like two hungry dogs baying for blood, taking it in turn to wield the one knife and plunge it into his body.

Bleeding badly, Archie tried to make a run for it but Paul and Vince were not going to let him off that lightly. They pulled him back and each took it in turn to stab him in the body, as deeply and painfully as possible.

The attack was becoming almost unreal in their minds but they could not stop themselves. They had lost control. The figure before them represented the lowest of the low. They felt no remorse. They just wanted revenge. This animal needed to be punished. They did not stop until he was dead.

Afterwards both men felt immensely satisfied. It was a good job well done. They had rid the world of a truly evil person and the rest of society should be grateful to them. Certainly, they had not intended actually to kill him, it just happened that way. In any case, Bigham was better off dead as far as they were concerned. Of course, the police did not see it quite like that.

Within days of detectives launching a murder hunt, they began to suspect that Karen was involved. Bigham's arrest record clearly related the assault on her, for which he had been prosecuted. Investigators started questioning her and people who knew her. It wasn't long before she was arrested. The police were sympathetic but she couldn't be allowed to get away with murder.

In March 1994, Karen, her brother Paul, Vince Scott and a friend called Gary Lee – who had disposed of the knife used to kill Bigham – appeared at the Old Bailey in London.

Karen, now aged eighteen and the mother of a nine-month-old baby, told the jury she didn't order her stepfather's death but had just wanted him beaten up.

'I blame myself because of the conversation I had with Vincent,' she confessed. 'I never told him to kill him. I told him I was upset that my stepfather had done it again.'

Karen denied aiding and abetting murder, and Vince Scott and Paul Bigham denied murder.

The jury accepted that none of the defendants had set out to murder Archie Bigham. Paul, now nineteen, was convicted of manslaughter and jailed for three and a half years. Vince was also convicted of manslaughter but was jailed for five years. Both were cleared of murder. Gary Lee was cleared of aiding and abetting murder and manslaughter and was placed on probation for two years after admitting disposing of the knife used to kill Archie.

Karen was led sobbing from the dock after being found guilty of aiding and abetting the manslaughter of her stepfather. She was jailed for a year.

During the hearing, prosecuting counsel David Spens told the court: 'In her eyes, the court which had put Archibald Bigham on probation had failed to stop him from doing it again.'

The Scapegoat

Sara Thornton threw the newspaper on the bed of her cell in a fury. She could not believe what she had just read. How could they? How could they? How could they free a man who admitted killing his wife?

She was serving a life sentence for an identical crime. The only difference was that she was a woman and her victim was a man.

Sara had been locked up inside Her Majesty's Prison Bullwood Hall, in Essex, for almost 18 months.

Her appeal against her sentence had just been turned down. Yet Joseph McGrail had kicked his frail wife to death and been allowed his liberty. It all seemed so unjust. So unfair. So inconsistent.

Sara faced a near lifetime in prison while Joseph MeGrail had walked to freedom from the very same Birmingham Crown Court where she had received her sentence. That made it even worse somehow The inconsistency of the law was one thing, but when the same court handed out two such entirely different punishments for basically the same crime it was a cruel double blow.

As she walked the jail corridors towards the refectory that afternoon she could not see or feel anything. Her mind was asking over and over again. Why? Why? Why?

'Hello Sara.'

Her fellow inmates might as well not have existed.

She did not hear them when they greeted her. They knew something must be wrong but they did not like to ask. The killers often got depressed. Who wouldn't if they faced half their life behind bars?

Sara took a small bowl from the pile of plates at the beginning of the food counter in the prison kitchen. She glanced past the hot, steaming overcooked meat. The broiled vegetables. The stinking fish. She stopped at the salad bar and picked at the lettuce, tomatoes and cucumbers on offer. They hardly looked appetising, but then Sara Thornton did not feel particularly hungry.

She looked at the rows of inmates sitting at the long refectory tables and realised she could not face a conversation with any of them. The strain of prison small talk was bad enough at the best of times, but she could not get her mind off Joseph McGrail. She did not even know the man. Not even what he looked like. But her thoughts were consumed by him. Why did he get freed when she was rotting in jail for an identical crime? Maybe he bribed the judge? Perhaps he begged for mercy? No. None of those reasons seemed entirely plausible. There was only one answer. It was because he was a man. That had to be the reason. What else could it possibly be?

Sara found herself just standing there with the salad bowl in her hand staring into oblivion.

'Are you sitting down or what?'

She snapped out of her self-induced trance the moment she heard that voice; It helped her decide. There was little pity between the four walls of a prison. Sara made up her mind there and then to do something about it. She wanted the world to know how unfair her sentence was. She walked back to her cell with that bowl of salad still gripped in one hand.

A few minutes later, she heard the ominous clank of her cell door locking. It was the beginning of the end of yet another horrible day.

As Sara lay on the wafer thin mattress of her cast iron bed, she started to cry. It was controllable at first. But then she just let the emotion take over. The earlier tension was being replaced by floods of fear and anxiety. There was now no light at the end of her tunnel. No hope for an early release from this hell on earth.

No one else did anything to try and console Sara that night as she sobbed into her pillow. She had no one to turn to except herself, inside that grim, soul-less place. Now she had run out of giving herself reassurance. There was nothing left.

On her bedside table, that bowl of salad lay untouched. Sara's appetite for all things had disappeared. She looked at the bowl for a moment and then sent it crashing to the cold stone floor. She decided there was one last way to force them to change their minds.

'It's your life Sara.'

The prison officer in charge of her block was not unsympathetic to Sara's plight. But when she announced she would be going on hunger strike in protest against her sentence it merely provoked a sigh of acceptance from prison staff members. After all, they had seen it all before.

Their main aim was to keep the inmates alive and healthy with the minimum of fuss. This was just another problem as far as they were concerned. And it was a problem they could have done without.

Back in her cell, Sara felt a fresh surge of energy. She had inspired herself by deciding to refuse food from then on. Now she had an aim in life – even though it could lead to her death.

A few days later, sitting at the tiny desk in her eight foot by eight foot cell, she started to write a letter to her 12-year-old daughter. The daughter she had been forced apart from 18 months earlier. The daughter she loved and cherished like no other human being. The daughter she so desperately wanted to see again.

Hello Darling,

It is Sunday morning. I feel fine, a little weak I guess. You do make me laugh when I tell you I am going on hunger strike, you tell me to take care of myself. Perhaps you don't quite understand. Either they let me free, or I will die. It is that simple, there are no alternatives.

I think I am forcing people to examine their own commitments to their lives. Just how many people know that things are wrong yet always find excuses not to do anything simply because it is the easier thing to go with the flow?

I feel weak, tired and bone cold but my spirit is strong. My skin is drying out. I'm going to end up just as one big wrinkle.

Sara Thornton put the pen down to rest a while. Her wrist ached from the pain of those words. She stretched and rolled her fingers to warm them against the cold. Then she shut her eyes and thought back to life in the outside world. Was it really that good?

Sara had felt something special toward Malcolm Thornton the first moment she had met him. He was such a nice bloke. Nothing was too much trouble for him. He'd been a policeman once. An upholder of the law. Sara was convinced that made him a fine, upstanding person. A man who could be trusted.

Malcolm was such a contrast from her earlier disastrous relationships. She was ecstatic when he asked her to marry him. She did not hesitate.

Their home in the picture postcard town of Atherstone, Warwickshire, looked like the perfect place for peace and harmony. But then appearances can be deceptive.

'You've got to come quickly doctor. I think he's going to kill me.'

Sara Thornton had been married to Malcolm for just a few weeks. Now she was at her wit's end. Her fine, upstanding husband was not just drunk. He was absolutely paralytic. As she put the phone down she turned to face the mounting fury of her beast of a husband. The very same man who had just a few weeks earlier promised to love and cherish her for the rest of his life was now smashing furniture to pieces. His eyes flared up in an alcoholic blurt when he spotted Sara. He had finished with the furniture. Now it was her turn.

When Dr Kenneth Farn got to the Thornton house on that hot summer's day in July, 1988, he was shocked. Sara was shaking with fear as the drunken lout who called himself her husband lay on the floor of their lounge gurgling and slurping uncontrollably. He looked like a beached whale. His time would come. His time would come.

'You have to sort yourself out Malcolm. You need treatment.'

Malcolm Thornton knew the doctor was right. But then he was sober now. You see, there were two Malcolm Thorntons. One was a funny, bright, witty man who would bowl people over with his generosity. The other Malcolm was like a raging wild animal destroying everything and everyone in his path. Sara Thornton knew both of them. She wished she did not.

But now the charming, reasonable Malcolm was facing up to the facts like a true man. He was an alcoholic and he accepted the fact. Dr Farn wanted to help his patient. Malcolm took his advice and headed for a specialist in London. Sara sighed with relief. He was doing something about it. He was a good man. He would sort himself out. She really wanted the loving, sweet Malcolm back forever.

By Christmas, 1988, Sara really thought she had got him back. 'Mr Hyde' had been beaten back into a shadowy past. And there, she was. The treatment had worked wonders. He was like a different man. She was so happy. So was her daughter Louise, aged 10. She wanted her mother to have the best in life. She deserved it.

Sara really felt true love for him. She had a reason to get up in the mornings. It felt so good to be so content. But it didn't last. It never does when you are dealing with the Malcolms of this world. There is always something lurking beneath the surface. That's why he had taken to the drink in the first place. There was a hidden motive behind his madness. Somewhere in there was a tortured soul desperate to get out. Alcohol was the only way it could manifest itself. It was his release from endless emotional torture. He could not hold it back for ever. Malcolm Thornton was the only person who really understood that.

'He's trying to kill me doctor. You've got to do something.'

Dr Farn was not surprised when he picked up the phone and Sara Thornton was on the line once more. In more than forty years as a GP, Malcolm Thornton was not the only alcoholic he had come across. Nevertheless, Dr Farn was still very concerned. His priority was the health and safety of Sara and Louise. He did not want to have a battered family on his conscience. Now he had a duty to protect his patients.

At the other end of the line, all hell was breaking loose in that pretty little house in the pretty little street in that pretty little town.

'Bitch. Uhm gunnuh kill you.'

Malcolm Thornton could barely speak the words coherently. But she knew exactly what he was saying. He was raving drunk. Completely out of control. He could have done anything to her. He didn't care.

But she still did not see his right hand clenching into a fist as his fury mounted. The first Sara knew about it was when she felt the knuckles crunch into her ribs. It was agonising. He had put his full, drunken force behind the punch and hit whatever he could focus on. It was easier than trying to aim at her face.

Thornton stumbled as he threw the punch into her stomach. It just made it worse. His full weight was behind it. There was no way to stop the double impact as his fist connected.

Sara doubled up in pain and collapsed to the floor of their lounge, clutching her stomach. It felt as if she had been turned inside out. She tried to push her stomach muscles outwards. The pain was appalling. The internal bruises had already begun.

He stood over her glaring, ready to follow up his assault with a flurry of punches. But there was no need. Sara would never recover.

'I want to kill him. I hate him.'

Sara Thornton knew she shouldn't have said it the moment she saw the reaction on her friend's face. She had spoken her mind once too often. Now was not the time to tell someone her feelings about her husband. It was better to keep everything bottled up inside herself. That way the hatred could fester and fester until she reached a point of no return. Pouring your problems out was too easy an answer to Sara's anguish. If she could rid herself of the hatred and fear just by telling a friend her innermost thoughts then life would be simple wouldn't it?

No. Society much preferred you to keep it all locked inside your brain. Never let it out to anyone. That way we might never know what awful thoughts you have. Basically, most people do not want to know what their friends are really thinking. It might be embarrassing. It might be shocking. It might be the truth.

As Sara quickly changed the subject following her candid disclosure, she realised that Malcolm Thornton was a problem she was going to have to sort out on her own. No one was going to help her. She would have to do it alone.

Malcolm Thornton's life was already falling apart without any assistance from his wife. He had lost his job after being breathalised. He had gone on a drinking spree following his release by the police. He had assaulted his wife. He had battered himself into submission.

What else did he have left in his life other than alcohol? It was his easiest form of escape. When the drink began to take effect he felt a surge of relief. He knew he could forget all his problems for a few hours and just soak himself in the dull throb of alcohol. The mortgage payments. The wife. No job. No future. Who gave a fuck? All those thoughts were left behind while he lapped up the beers and spirits that had become his staple diet in life.

The pubs were like a separate world for Malcolm Thornton. No one bothered him. He could talk to who he liked when he liked. If he wanted to sit in the corner and sup silently he could. If he wanted to talk to his drinking partners about football and women he could. It was his choice. It was his way out.

Meanwhile at home, Sara was at the end of her tether. Her husband – the man whom she so adored when they married just a few months earlier – had now become an out and out failure. No job. No income. No love. No life. And no future for them.

He had put paid to that and she hated him for it. How could he destroy everything around him?

It was all such a waste.

She sat and watched the television but she did not know what was on the screen. Her mind was a million light years away from that programme. She was contemplating the future and it looked bleak.

She had to talk to someone about it all. But who? Her friend had not been interested. Her daughter was too young. Who could she turn to? But Sara already knew the answer: No one. She had to deal with this herself. If she did not then no one else would.

She went up to bed alone as usual that night. He would appear eventually. Too drunk to take off his clothes let alone give her the love and attention she so craved. Sara took out her lipstick and sat looking into the bedroom mirror for a few moments. She rocked back and forth gently yet tensely and shut her eyes and let her mind wander.

At first they were good thoughts. Louise playing in the garden, wide-eyed, face smiling. Other children looking happy and so contented. Then *he* came on the scene. She could see his face angrily close up against her own. He was shouting abuse at her. Then he threw a punch.

She snapped out of her day dream and looked in the mirror once more. All she could see was a desperately unhappy face, lined with fear and misery. Sara twisted the bottom of the canister of lipstick so that the red tip slowly grew longer. She studied it for a second. Then she put it between her fingers like a pen and began to write on the mirror in front of their bed:

'Bastard Thornton. I hate you.'

Sara did not go to bed that night after all. It was still early. She was not going to give him the pleasure of knowing she would be waiting obediently in bed for his return. That had happened on too many occasions in the past.

This time she was going to surprise him. Sara tidied herself in front of that same mirror where she had just scrawled her desperate message of hate and walked out of the front door.

This time she was going to have a drink. She had been through enough. Why couldn't she enjoy herself for once. But Sara did not like being out for long. Within an hour she was back at the neatly kept house. He wasn't there. She felt so disappointed. She had hoped that perhaps he would get back and find her gone and start to think about the consequences of his actions.

But he had gone past the point of no return. He did not care. As she sat there downstairs in the tiny living room, she heard him scraping the front door lock with his key. She did not need to even see him to know he was drunk. Probably so inebriated he could not get that key in the lock at the first, second or even third attempt.

It must have taken ten goes before the key connected and the drunken mess stumbled through the doorway. He stood there for a moment and just stared at her. She wondered if perhaps he felt a twinge of guilt. Maybe even a little shame?

But Malcolm Thornton did not feel anything of the kind. His only thoughts were filled with hate. She seemed to be smirking at him. Making fun of him. Trying to make him feel guilty.

'What's your problem?'

He did not really care. He just did not like being made to feel bad. But he would get his own back on her.

'Just come to bed Malcolm.'

Sara had given up on her husband. The message written on the mirror upstairs said it all. She wanted him to know how much hatred she felt towards him. He had made her life a misery. He had destroyed her future. What more could he do? Now he lay slumped on their sofa. A drunken hulk of a man once again incapacitated by the alcohol he craved for. Malcom Thornton wanted to escape. Soon he would escape for good.

'Well. I'm going to bed.'

Sara did not really know why she bothered saying the words. He was still collapsed on the sofa. He mumbled some obscenity at her but his lips could not keep pace with his brain. He was out of sync. When he spoke it was like an actor in one of those badly dubbed foreign films. His mind was filled with evil thoughts but he was having immense difficulties making his mouth work accordingly.

Then she heard the unmistakable words. The utterance that was totally unforgivable in her terms. The threat that shook her into action. So vicious that it convinced her utterly that he was no better than scum.

'Keep that daughter of yours out of my way or else she'll be dead meat.'

There was no mistaking his words. He had paused long and hard before saying it. No doubt he wanted to make sure he did not suffer his usual lip synch problems. He was determined to ensure that she heard it all.

'Keep that daughter of yours out of my way or else she'll be dead meat.'

Sara sat there in silence. She absorbed the words slowly. She could not comprehend it at first. What did her 10-year-old daughter have to do with their problems? Why was he dragging her into this?

When it dawned on her, she was barely able to contain herself. She clenched both her hands into tight fists, struggling to stop her finger nails digging too deeply into the palms of her hands.

How dare he threaten my daughter. My only reason for living. My only happiness. My only joy.

Now she really understood him for the first time. Through all his dozens of drinking sessions and abuse he had never tried to involve Louise. Now he had crossed that final barrier. This was worse than all-out war. This was a warning about the safety of her only piece of true flesh and blood. He was putting her life at risk. He was daring to suggest that Louise could be in danger from him – the only other person living in that tiny house. Malcolm Thornton made it sound like he was pronouncing a death sentence on Louise. Actually, he was helping to guarantee his own.

'You fucking whore.'

Sara's drunken slob of a husband had just got a second wind. The tirade of insults that followed were far more audible than his earlier words. He had seen the look of shock and horror on her face after he made that threat to her daughter. Now he was going in for the kill with a flurry of blue obscenities that turned the atmosphere real.

Sara still sat there totally stunned by his bullying tactics. She wasn't really listening to the tirade of verbal abuse. Her mind was on one person – her darling little daughter who lay asleep just a few feet away. What if he meant it? What if he really did intend to do her harm? How could they live under the same roof with that threat hanging over? He was calling her little baby 'dead meat'. Sara was not going to risk it. She had to do something.

'Whore! Whore! Whore!'

Sara's silence seemed to inspire Malcolm Thornton to even nastier language. He was shouting at the top of his voice now. But the only words she heard were:

'Keep that daughter of yours out of my way or else

she'll be dead meat.' This bastard was going to kill her daughter unless she did something. He was going to butcher her beautiful little girl. One day, when she was out he would creep up on Louise and murder her. But he would only be doing it to get at his wife. Louise would end up being the innocent victim of her mother's hatred for her husband.

Sara hated the feeling that she was responsible. It made her realise she had to act – fast!

She got up without saying a word and walked into the kitchen. The drunken lump was still continuing his stream of obscenities. He was oblivious to the fact she had left the room. He did not care. He just wanted to hurt her and Louise.

In the kitchen, she opened a drawer and found what she was looking for. It was one of their very best steak knives. Malcolm always wanted the best. Now he was going to get it. First she had to make sure it was going to do the job properly. Sara pulled out the knife sharpener and began, almost lovingly to scrape the knife over the rough edged metal. Each time, she would gently rub her thumb across the edge to see if it was definitely sharp enough. Finally, it was ready. In the lounge, Thornton was still shouting. But Sara had heard it all before. She was not going to hear it much longer.

She looked down at him one last time. She glanced at his bloated beer-filled stomach with disdain. He had dared to threaten the life of her daughter. Now he would pay the price.

But did she really want to kill him? Did she honestly want to take another person's life? Sara Thornton did not really know the answer to that herself. She stood with the specially sharpened knife waiting. Perhaps he would grab it off her? At least he would ward her off surely?

It was possible that for one strange moment she hoped he would stop her. After all, killing is not an easy task for anyone. It takes a lot of courage, fear and hatred.

She could not wait a moment longer. She plunged the knife into his soft protruding stomach and dug the six-inch blade in as far as it would go.

Suddenly a frenzy took over. She started to stab and stab and stab. Nothing could stop her now. The killing was done. Little Louise could live safely. He wouldn't get to her. He was not going to harm her.

'I've just killed my husband. I've stuck a six-inch carving knife in his belly.'

It was a matter-of-fact statement, with no emotion except, perhaps for a faint air of resignation.

Sara did not bother to wait until the emergency services arrived to make her confession. She told the operator after she had dialled 999. She had nothing to hide. She felt no shame. In fact she felt relief from the awful burden of living with a bullying brute who had plagued every working moment of her existence.

Still she felt as if she needed further reassurance. She went to a cupboard and took out a camera. She wanted to record her husband's final dying moments. She wanted to have a record of the terror she had inflicted on him after years of being on the receiving end.

Sara looked at the bloody corpse of her 44-year-old husband through the view-finder of the camera and pressed the shutter tight.

Click. She captured his dying moments.

Click. She watched as he bled to death.

Click. She saw him get exactly what he deserved.

The ambulancemen who showed up were astonished when they saw her taking the pictures. She couldn't give a damn. She just hoped that the judge would understand all the pain and suffering she had endured at her husband's hands.

In HM Prison Bullwood Hall more than two years later, Sara had discovered that there was no sympathy for a woman who kills her husband.

It was August 10, 1991, and 34-year-old Sara was frail and weak from the hunger strike she vowed would continue until the Home Secretary promised to re-examine her case.

'I have no wish to die. I love life too much. But I cannot let this issue pass without making a stand. My life is all I have left to fight for.'

The judge at her trial at Birmingham Crown Court had not appreciated the pain and suffering she had endured. Sentencing her to life imprisonment, Mr Justice Igor Judge told Sara: 'You have been convicted of murder. The law permits only one sentence for murder, that you go to prison for life.'

In July 1991, her attempt to overturn the murder conviction in the Appeal Court had failed.

The hunger strike was Sara's last resort.

As her supporters waved placards and demanded a re-trial outside the prison, Sara doggedly refused to take my food for 20 days. She only decided to give up her fast when she was reunited with her daughter Louise who had moved to America to live with Sara's sister after her imprisonment.

'My daughter and I have a deep and unique relationship. If I die she won't have a mother.'

The Home Secretary has so far rejected all appeals for the case to be re-examined. Meanwhile, the campaign to free Sara goes on.

Wife killer Joe McGrail remains a free man.

Ma Baker

Male nurse Leonard Rose hated working the night shift at the Clarke Institute of Psychiatry, in Toronto, Canada. It was not an easy place at the best of times, but there was something about the night-time that brought out the worst in some of the more difficult patients. His rounds at the hospital includes the carefully segregated male and female wards. Each hour, he would quietly patrol the immaculately clean corridors that were separated by a pair of swing doors.

It was a tedious task in many ways but it had to be done, otherwise all sorts of dangerous scenarios could occur.

The Clarke – as it was known locally – was filled with a bizarre mish-mash of inmates ranging from convicted criminals judged to be bordering on insanity, to voluntary patients trying to prevent themselves from sliding into serious psychiatric problems. The stresses and strains of living in the modern world had proved too much for many of these individuals. Some were, inevitably, victims – abused as children, driven to commit crimes because of their own lack of self-esteem, sexual perverts with no other place to turn.

On a hot summer's night in August, 1986, Nurse Leonard Rose was more concerned with maintaining a quiet life, if you can call working in a psychiatric hospital that. As the sun rose and early morning rays peeped through the wafer-thin hospital curtains, Leonard began his sixth and final tour of the wards before finishing his shift. He was really looking forward to getting home to a hearty breakfast and a few hours' sleep.

As was his usual procedure, Leonard began his round by checking through the forensic unit of the hospital. By the time he got to the main men's ward, it was around 7am. All was quiet – if anything, too quiet. He cast his eyes along the row of beds on each side of the ward to make sure everyone was accounted for. Suddenly, Nurse Rose did a double take. One of the inmates was absent from his bed. He walked briskly towards the empty bed, just to make sure he was right. But there was absolutely no sign of Bruce Lynch – a convicted armed robber, who was considered a 'high-security' inmate even by Clarke standards.

Nurse Rose rushed to the men's room and methodically checked each cubicle to see if Lynch was there but somehow he knew, even before he entered the bathroom, that the inmate would be nowhere in sight. Leonard remembered that another nurse had told him about problems they had encountered involving an illicit romance between Lynch and a female inmate called Harriet Giesecke.

He dashed over to the female ward, convinced that they were up to something. He cast his eyes along the row of beds in room 401 to see if Giesecke was there. She was nowhere to be spotted. He walked towards her bed, looking for clues.

Harriet Giesecke and Bruce Lynch could hardly contain their giggles as they lay naked beneath that very same bed. Nurse Leonard was carrying out a frantic search for them but they did not give a damn. Instead, Harriet opened her legs even wider so that Lynch could penetrate deeper into her.

She bit into his shoulder to stop Nurse Rose from hearing her moans of pleasure. Her hands slapped and pinched his bottom before pulling him even deeper into her. She could feel his tongue exploring the cavities of her ear. Neither of them cared that just a few feet away were dozens of female inmates and Nurse Rose. Maybe it was out and out exhibitionism. Or perhaps they were simply so desperate to seal their love for one another that they had to do it anywhere, any place.

Whatever the reason, no one was about to stop 30-year-old Harriet Giesecke from getting exactly what she wanted. As she lay there, legs spread wide apart under that rusting metal hospital bed, her thoughts were consumed by one, overriding emotion – passion. As she got closer and closer to a climax, so the fear of being caught subsided to the point where she did not care.

Harriet bit deep into Lynch's shoulder at the moment of ultimate satisfaction. She could not stop herself thrusting her hips up towards him in an effort to squeeze every drop of excitement out of their embrace.

She was virtually oblivious to the world when Nurse Leonard Rose stooped down and peered under the bed, having at last found his two missing inmates.

'Stop it now!' Rose yelled so loud that many of the patients woke with a start. The ones who had already been fully conscious just sniggered as they watched Harriet's white quivering knees still spread apart by a man's bottom thrusting up and down.

Bruce Lynch, aged 25, hesitantly withdrew from Harriet and climbed out from under the bed, looking a bit sheepish to say the least. As he stood up next to Nurse Rose and wrapped a hospital dressing-gown around himself, he looked down at Harriet, still lying spread-eagled on the cold vinyl floor, and smiled. It was a smile that could best be described as being very similar to that of a cat that just drank it's last drop of cream from a plate.

'Come on. Get up now!'

Nurse Rose was in no mood to be sensitive to Harriet's embarrassing position. But then Harriet did not seem that bothered either. She ever so casually got up from the floor and brushed past the male nurse, much to the amusement of virtually every other inmate in room 401 that morning.

But Bruce Lynch was not the only man in the Clarke Institute who was madly in love with Harriet Giesecke. Her brown, wavy hair and neat facial features certainly distinguished her from most of the worn, thin, haggard female faces in that daunting hospital. She had quickly caught the eye of Ron Nicholl, another seasoned criminal bordering on the insane. He and Lynch became known as Harriet's 'boys' and, perhaps not so surprisingly, she soon got nicknamed 'Ma Baker'.

Harriet had voluntarily checked herself in to the Clarke Institute to try and sort out various 'psychiatric problems' that had troubled her for many years and led her into a lot of minor trouble with the law.

But the truth was that she probably rather enjoyed life inside the Clarke's four walls because it was a world where responsibilities were kept to a minimum. You didn't need money, there were no bills, there was little emotion. It was simple, really; you did pretty well what you liked, within the confines of a hospital filled to the brim with seriously disturbed people. To Harriet even that bizarre world was preferable to life on the outside – she had left her husband Randy and their baby daughter Erica many months previously and just ended up drifting from job to job and bed to bed. Now, in the Clarke, none of those problems were weighing her down. Her biggest dilemma was when to check out of the hospital and face the outside world once more.

She had gradually built up a loathing and hatred towards her husband for kicking her out and taking her pretty little daughter away from her. Doctors said it was these problems that drove Harriet into the arms of renegades like Lynch and Nicholl. Relatives and friends said it was purely down to her insatiable appetite for sex. Whatever the truth, Harriet Giesecke had a fairly outrageous reputation at the Clarke, especially after that sex incident under the bed with Lynch.

Harriet loved the attention all the men were constantly giving her. She adored to feel them lusting after her as she swaggered her shapely hips along the corridors of the Clarke. She knew that patients and staff alike were all well aware of her sexual promiscuity and that made her feel good. She had spent her entire life longing for love and attention. In that grim, grey place she was getting huge doses of that.

But Harriet also had another motive for flirting

with Nicholl and Lynch. In her role as 'Ma Baker', she wanted to persuade them to commit a crime so horrendous that it would affect them all for the rest of their living days.

'I'll give you $5,000 – cash.'

Lynch and Nicholl listened open-mouthed as the woman they both lusted after so much made them an astonishing offer to murder her husband Randy.

Harriet Giesecke wanted the two hard men to kill her husband because she was determined to stop him having sole custody of their child.

'He beat me so bad that I had to leave the house, but he's still got my daughter and God knows what he's doin' to her.'

It was a fairly convincing story. But, all the same, Harriet was trying to hire two men to commit the ultimate crime. It was not a decision that any person could take lightly.

'Why don't you just take off with the baby? Seems much easier than murder to me.'

Ron Nicholl seemed to be making much more sense than Harriet. But the attractive brunette just could not see it that way.

'The cops'll come after me. I'll never get far. No. Killin' him's much easier.'

Nicholl did not reply. He watched as his love rival Bruce Lynch nodded his head hesitantly. At that moment Ron Nicholl decided it was time to split from 'Ma Baker' and her 'boys.' Murder was not something he wanted to get involved in.

Harriet Giesecke was disappointed but not put off by Nicholl's refusal to get involved. She resolved there and then to check out of the Clarke Institute and wait for her lover Lynch to get out, so they could commit the perfect crime together.

Randy Giesecke had been heartbroken when his marriage to Harriet crumbled. They had met a few years earlier when he was married to another woman and he'd given up his family and a safe, comfortable, suburban life to be with the intelligent Harriet. She had swept him off his feet with her sensuous advances. She had told him about her rich parents and the luxury lifestyle she had enjoyed as a kid growing up in Michigan. It all seemed like a fairy-tale romance during those first few happy months, but the cracks soon began to appear in their relationship.

To begin with, Randy – a 31-year-old life insurance salesman – discovered that his new wife's claims of great wealth were no more than a huge sham. The truth was far more hard for him to swallow – she was a convicted petty criminal with a long record of problems with the police.

Then she got pregnant and Randy hoped that this might help Harriet to settle down to a normal life. He genuinely wanted their marriage to work and was delighted when she announced she was pregnant. Maybe a child might help heal their rocky relationship.

But the truth was that the birth of beautiful little

Erica in April, 1985, provided no more than a brief respite from Harriet's outrageous activities. Within a few weeks of her birth, the couple were arguing virtually every minute of the day. Most of the rows were about money. The problem was that Harriet had set herself up in such a bizarre fantasy world of the rich and famous that she could not handle the reality of the situation, which was that they were a financially stretched young family. Just like everyone else. But Harriet could not accept that. She didn't want to be normal. It was dull. It lacked edge.

It was no real surprise to Randy or his parents when Harriet stormed out of their modest home in Scarborough, just north-east of Toronto. And the bitter custody battle for little Erica that followed was something that, sadly, millions of couples throughout the world seem to experience after the break up of a marriage. But that did not make it any less painful for either of the heartbroken parents. Randy, the responsible one with the safe job and the steady reputation, against Harriet, the fantasy merchant with a criminal record as long as her arm – it was hardly surprising when the courts looked set to award Randy full custody of the child. But, tragically, Harriet's fear of that decision probably contributed most of all to his eventual brutal departure from this earth.

The custody split sparked a feeling of overwhelming bitterness inside Harriet's mind. She felt betrayed by the system, even though in reality she never stood the remotest chance of gaining the right to bring up her own daughter. She convinced herself that it was all a conspiracy against her. She felt trapped in a world where she had nothing to offer. The pride had dropped out of her life. As the bitterness mounted, so her animal cunning began to take over the logical parts of her mind.

Even after she moved in with her husband's aunt, who was supposed to be a calming influence, the anger and resentment just continued to build within her.

One day, when her husband came by his aunt's to pick up Erica after a rare visit to her mother, Harriet followed him home to ensure she had an address for her estranged husband. She had been barred by the court from being allowed to know his address because there were genuine fears she might snatch the child. But that was not her intention in following Randy home. She was laying the seeds for a death trap. But her plans had only just begun ...

Randy Giesecke was never one to ignore an opportunity to earn a little extra commission in his job as a life insurance salesman. So when a man called Mike Simmons rang him up and asked him if he'd come round to give him and his wife Susan a quote later that day, Randy was only too delighted to oblige.

The address Mr Simmons gave was 164 Hollyberry Trail. If only Randy had realised that it did not exist. But then Harriet Giesecke simply wanted to lure her estranged husband to the street where her lover lived and then blast him to bits for ever.

'I should be back in about an hour.'

Randy Giesecke was leaving instructions for the baby-sitter at the immaculate flat he lived in with baby daughter Erica, when the phone rang. It was 'Mr Simmons' again, cancelling their arrangement. Randy was disappointed. He had been hoping to sign up the Simmonses for a really hefty life insurance policy, and that would have helped pay for some special new clothes for his beloved Erica. He had no idea that the second 'Mr Simmons' call was also a phoney – investigated by Harriet after she realised that she could not cold-bloodedly kill her husband in the street. She would have to think of some other way of trapping him in a dark and isolated spot ...

Harriet Giesecke knew precisely where her husband parked his Ford pick-up truck in the underground car park to the apartment block where he lived. She quietly pulled her own car to a halt in the space next to his and switched off the engine and waited. It was September 22, 1986, just a few days away from that final custody hearing that would confirm all her worst fears. Harriet Giesecke sat there patiently, in no particular hurry She could wait He would come home from work eventually, and then she would get him.

She felt the excitement working through her system. She clutched the sawn-off shotgun between her legs, switched on the radio cassette and pressed fast forward until she found her favourite song. She did not care how long it would take. She was not even worried that the silver Honda Accord she was driving had been stolen by her lover Lynch from an ex-girlfriend of his. The cops were hardly likely to patrol an underground car park.

It was 6.30pm. Harriet nuzzled the warm wooden handle of that shotgun against herself and pressed her legs together tightly, in anticipation of what was about to happen. It was a strange sensation – a blend of fear and excitement that was working its way through her. She rocked back and forth in time to the heavy metal music on the cassette and shut her eyes for a few moments. She could see the happy, smiling face of her daughter now. She could see them all together in happier days. She wished she could turn the clock back but it was too late.

Harriet's trance was broken by the screech of a tyre on the dry surface of that car park. It was followed by the deep revving noise of a powerful V8 engine. Then the tyres screeched again as the car headed up the ramp towards where she was parked. Her eyes squinted against the glare of the vehicle's full-beam headlamps. Then she made him out, sitting behind the wheel of that pick-up. It was her husband Randy.

She exited the Honda silently and swiftly. So fast, in fact, that her husband had only one foot on the ground when he saw his wife.

Her finger was itching to press the trigger. But she wanted to take one long last look at him before she said goodbye for ever.

No words were exchanged between them. Harriet

just saw him pan down to the shotgun in her hand and mouth the word 'No!'. That was all he had time to do before she allowed that itchy finger to get on with what it wanted to do.

She aimed right at his heart. It had to be the best place to start with. Harriet felt the weapon jolt in her hand as she fired. It must have lifted up a full five inches after the first cartridge shot out of the stubby barrel she bad so painstakingly sawn down a few days earlier.

Randy Giesecke was thrown back a good three feet by the force of that first shot. It seared into his chest – a spray of tiny fragments of metal, each one piercing its own hole in the flesh. Instinctively, he put his right hand up to feel the gaping wound. If he had looked down at that moment he would have seen his shredded heart, barely pumping and exposed through the shattered remains of his chest.

Harriet Giesecke walked towards her husband then, determined to get a better aim before she blasted him into eternity. He was half-standing as the blood poured rapidly out of him. But she was not close enough yet.

Randy Giesecke looked up at the approaching death machine and let his eyelids flutter in resignation. He knew the end was very near. Now he just wanted her to get on with it, for he could not stand the pain a moment longer. All he could really see were the two barrels getting nearer and nearer. Harriet wanted him to suffer. Her upper lip curled as she witnessed his pain. So good to see. It inspired her to let that index finger do its job once again. This time the shot ripped open a hole in his head the size of a golfball.

Harriet headed for the Honda Accord. Just five floors above them in the same apartment block, little Erica was playing with her teddy bears as the baby-sitter watched the seven o'clock TV news.

Harriet Giesecke put on a marvellous performance at her slain husband's funeral in the nearby town of North York. The eyes of all his relatives were upon her as they lowered his body into the ground a week after what the newspapers called a 'senseless, coldblooded robbery attempt that had gone tragically wrong'.

She was enjoying every minute of their suffering. At least now Randy would not get to have custody of Erica, even if she was still deemed far too irresponsible to look after the child herself.

As she drove away from the funeral, having been snubbed by all her husband's relatives, Harriet was feeling good about life for the first time in years. If she had paid better attention to her rear-view mirror, she might have seen the two plain-clothes-police squad cars following her through the streets of North York.

She did not even notice them when she stopped in Edwards Gardens, walked over to an empty bench and waited for her secret lover to turn up for a clandestine meeting.

Across the street, Bruce Lynch walked casually towards her without even bothering to question why two saloon cars, each filled with three men, were stationed just a hundred yards from where his girlfriend was patiently waiting.

The detectives could not believe their luck. All fingers were pointing towards Harriet Giesecke as the main suspect in the murder of her husband, but so far they did not have a shred of evidence against her. As the officers watched the so-called grieving widow sitting with a man on that wooden bench, passionately kissing him, their eyebrows arched and they knew they were onto something.

Harriet, for her part, was just relieved to be close to Bruce once more. Their illicit sex sessions in places as obscure as the floor under her bed when they were together in the Clarke Institute were now just a fond memory. As she felt his lips kissing her neck, she wished she could just pull him down on top of her in that very public place. But not even Harriet Giesecke could bring herself to be that outrageous.

As she ran her fingers through his thick black hair, she could not wait to get him to herself. It would not be long, and then they could be together for ever.

The detectives witnessing the couple's passion on that bench were intrigued. What was Harriet doing with a parole violator with a long history of armed robbery? They knew there and then that it would only be a matter of time before they arrested Harriet Giesecke for the murder of her husband.

And Harriet's romantic escapades on a park bench were not the only interesting facts unearthed by detectives over the next few days. A cashier at a sports shop in the nearby Newtonbrook Plaza recalled Harriet coming into the store looking for a high-powered magnum 'Dirty Harry' special, plus ammunition, to hunt 'big game'. That was just a few days before the murder of Randy Giesecke.

Then a nursery-school teacher came forward to tell cops that she had seen Harriet Giesecke driving a car into the underground car park of the apartment block where her husband and daughter lived. She recalled the precise time – it had been 6.15pm, about an hour before Randy was blasted to death so cold-bloodedly.

The jigsaw was complete when police searched the flat Harriet shared with her lover Bruce and found a saw and fragments of metal that came from the remains of the shotgun when she cut it down for maximum killing potential.

Two months after her husband's vicious slaying, Harriet Giesecke was arrested and charged with his murder.

On the last day of the trial, June 18, 1988, Giesecke was so confident she would be found not guilty that she turned to one of the cops guarding her, held up her handcuffed wrists and said: 'This is the last time you'll be putting these cuffs on me.'

After the jury deliberated for more than four days, Giesecke was astonished to be found guilty of first-degree murder. Her lover Bruce Lynch was acquitted of all involvement in the crime.

Harriet Giesecke is currently serving her life sentence in the Kingston Penitentiary for Women, with no eligibility for parole for at least twenty-five years. Ironically, her lover Bruce Lynch is serving a ten-year sentence for robbery and theft at the nearby Joyceville Penitentiary.

The couple were given special permission to marry in June, 1989, in Harriet's prison. Authorities were especially amazed by their decision to wed because Harriet had tried to implicate Lynch in the murder of her husband.

But, every six weeks, armed guards bring Lynch to visit Harriet at her jail and they are allowed to spend at least two hours in a trailer in the prison grounds. It is believed the couple enjoy a full marriage.

Meanwhile, Harriet's daughter Erica – now 7-years-old – is living happily and securely with Randy Giesecke's parents in Toronto. Harriet has told people she misses her daughter 'very much' but it is unlikely they will ever meet again if the Gieseckes have any say in the matter.

The Root of all Evil

The noise of aircraft taking off from nearby Heathrow Airport every thirty seconds is the sound that dominates life in Hounslow, Middlesex. It is a somewhat sad, sprawling concrete jungle of high-rise estates and tatty between-the-wars housing that can be seen from any aircraft approaching Britain's busiest travel centre.

Not surprisingly, property prices have always been fairly reasonable in Hounslow. It is stuck in that no man's land between the city and the countryside. And, for that reason, it became probably one of the most popular areas in Britain for the teeming masses of Asian immigrants who flooded into the country in the fifties and sixties.

These were hard-working people who dreamt of opening shops and businesses, and living the sort of lifestyles many of them knew they could never attain in their homeland. And certainly, without the hundreds of thousands of immigrants from countries like India and Pakistan, this country's individually owned shops might have become a thing of the past, as the huge supermarket chains swallowed up customers at an alarming rate.

So, the majority of shops in Hounslow were naturally owned by those very same hard-working Asians. Many of these businesses stayed open virtually throughout the night and, as a result, earned their owners healthy profits compared with their British predecessors, who tended to run rigid nine-to-five operations.

The other reason why the Asian population of places like Hounslow did such good business was that most of their shops were manned by members of their own families. Wives, sons, daughters, mothers and fathers were all expected to do their stint behind the counter. These shopkeepers were never saddled with the expense of hiring staff – they were already living on the premises.

Mohinder Cheema was one such classic example

of a successful Asian businessman in Hounslow. Since arriving in Britain in the fifties, he had gradually bought up an off-licence, two shops and a host of other residential property at a time when prices were but a mere fraction of what they are today.

But no one – not even his attractive dark-haired wife Julie – knew exactly how much Mohinder Cheema was worth. The 54-year-old businessman kept things close to his chest. It was frustrating for all those around him, like Julie and the three children they had between them. But that was the way Mohinder had always operated and nothing was going to change his habit of a lifetime.

Sometimes, 44-year-old Julie Cheema wondered why she had married her husband in the first place. Their romance and eventual wedding in 1985 had surprised both their families. He was the frail, yet astute millionaire who had carefully and patiently nurtured a whole range of businesses in the area. She came from a much more traditional British background and many people found it hard to imagine what on earth they could have in common.

But Julie was very taken with her husband at first. He had a wonderful eye for a deal. An ability to make money out of nothing, and she really respected that skill in any man. But that kind of admiration is not usually enough to keep a marriage intact.

There was another side to her husband that most women would find hard to cope with. The physical side of their relationship was virtually non-existent. Mohinder Cheema suffered from chronic asthma and frequently had to retire to bed when his breathing became seriously affected.

At first, Julie was a sympathetic nurse. Helping and understanding her husband's obvious suffering. But after a few years of marriage, she started to resent the constant interruptions to her life. She longed for the physical side of their marriage to get going now and again. But somehow she knew that they could never have a normal marriage in the accepted sense. Julie Cheema began to look elsewhere for affection.

Neil Marklew was a gangly youth of just 19 when he first met Julie. To begin with, this unlikely twosome became genuine friends. There was no physical bond between them. After all, he was twenty-five years younger than her. But, despite the age difference, Neil and Julie had a lot in common. He lived with his parents in Catherine Gardens, just around the corner from the Cheemas' main off-licence in Cromwell Road, Hounslow.

Naturally, they met when he used to pop into the shop for some ice-cold beers to take home. The first few times they had just exchanged pleasantnes. He did not even really notice her hand brush his as she gave him change. He certainly did not realise that she was building him up into the object of her desires.

But then Julie Cheema did not have much else in her life at that time. Her husband was becoming more and more short-tempered as his asthma attacks became increasingly regular.

However, there was an even more disturbing development in the Cheema household: Mohinder Cheema was beginning to make all sorts of thinly veiled threats to his wife about cutting her out of his will. He might have been a sick man, but he knew full well that his wife was not truly in love with him. His children from his earlier marriage did not get on with her and they kept warning him. Inevitably, he began to take heed of their advice. He started to question her motives in even having married him in the first place. He wondered what her real intentions were.

The relationship between Julie and her husband had reached an all-time low by the summer of 1990. Business might have been going extremely well in the Cheema store, but life at home was just one long round of arguments and tension. Mohinder Cheema was spending much of his time in bed and his wife was trying to stay out of the house as frequently as possible.

Then one day she came home early and was about to enter his bedroom when she heard voices. It was one of his grown-up sons. She stopped in her tracks and waited and listened. The voices were loud and clear. They were discussing Mohinder's will, and it was becoming perfectly clear that there were plans afoot to cut Julie out of it.

She waited a few moments longer and then

silently tiptoed away. She did not want them to know she had been listening, because she was about to hatch a plan that had to be completely foolproof.

Neil Marklew knew that Julie Cheema had a soft spot for him and he was enjoying the attention of an older woman. They would meet in the middle of the day whilst her husband was working in the shop. Neil – unemployed – enjoyed their little love trysts because it broke up the monotony of his life on the dole. The days were the most boring time of all because so many of his mates were either at college or out working.

During that hot summer of 1990, they met in parks, pubs and coffee shops to talk about life, love and Mohinder Cheema. Julie seemed almost obsessed with her husband and his plans to cut her out of the will. She knew he had not done it yet, but she firmly believed it would happen. She knew full well that her husband was watching her every move. He suspected she was getting physical gratification from elsewhere. The truth was that Julie had not committed adultery – yet. She was more content just having a companion to confide in, even if he was young enough to be her son.

But, as is so often the case, teenager Neil Marklew's affection for Julie was growing by the day. He found himself thinking about her virtually every waking moment. The more they met and talked, the more he began to want her all to himself. Yet, up until then, they had done nothing more than kiss on street corners and stroke hands over the tops of coffee-shop tables.

Virtually no one knew about their secret liaisons. Neil knew that his mates would rib him mercilessly if they found out, and Julie certainly had no intention of telling a living soul. But Neil was starting to feel completely swept up by her. He was prepared to do anything to encourage their love – her wishes were his commands.

'I'd kill him for you if you asked me.'

Neil Marklew was fooling around with his 44-year-old sweetheart. He just wanted to show her how much he cared for her. But Julie Cheema took it all the wrong way.

'Do you mean that?'

The teenager hesitated for a moment and looked into Julie Cheema's eyes. He had a horrible feeling she was taking him seriously. But he wanted to show her just how tough he was – it was the biggest mistake he ever made in his entire life.

'Sure I do,' he mumbled. But she took no notice of his reticence.

'I hate him, you know. I've been thinking of killing him for ages but I don't know how.'

Neil Marklew had opened up a whole can of worms and now he was discovering what it would take to win Julie's love for ever.

He sat there nodding his head as she took a deep breath and carried on: 'There must be a way we could do it.'

Neil was starting to get used to the idea. He began to realise that this might be a way out of the doldrums of unemployment. His love for her was blinded by emotion. Just so long as they were careful, then why should they get caught?

'Well, it'll cost you.'

'How much do you think?'

'You tell me – what's he worth?'

'Five million.'

Neil let out a long whistle. He had no idea his sweetheart's husband was worth that sort of money.

'I'd just be happy to run the off-licence.'

'Okay. It's yours if you do the job properly.'

The truth was that Julie Cheema had always had an inflated opinion of her husband's real wealth. But to her, one off-licence seemed a small price to pay compared to the five million pounds she believed he was worth in total. In reality, it was about one fifth of that sum.

'Right, give me some money and I'll get a gun.' Neil also knew just the bloke for this job of assassin.

Robert Naughton, aged 20, was desperate for money. Like his friend Neil Marklew, he was also unemployed but he did not have the luxury of his parents to fall back on. He needed cash fast and when his pal suggested a 'little job' he did not hesitate. Even when Neil passed him the sawn-off shotgun and told him the victim was his sweetheart's husband, he did not bat an eyelid.

As far as Naughton was concerned, it would be a 'piece of cake'. The two friends finished off their pints of bitter in their local tavern and walked out to prepare for the job that they hoped would set them up with a business for life.

'Bang. Bang.' Neil turned to his pal: 'It'll be as easy as that.'

It was a pretty hot day in Hounslow in August, 1990. Business in cold drinks was brisk at the Cheemas' off-licence in Cromwell Road and Mohinder Cheema must have been hoping the good weather would continue.

He and his wife were both in the shop during the late afternoon that day, as was so often the case. Julie was giving the place a good clean and her husband was sitting – due to his bad health – behind the counter of the shop.

Neither of them paid much attention to a gangly youth who walked in. Perhaps if they had bothered to look at him a bit sooner, they would have noticed that he was wearing a heavy coat despite the scorching hot weather.

By the time Robert Naughton pulled out his shotgun, it was too late.

The first shower of metal hit Mohinder Cheema in the side of his chest. As he keeled over on the floor, Naughton pointed and fired a second time. On this occasion, the fragments of shot somehow missed most of their target except for Mohinder Cheema's fingers. Doctors later found lots of pieces of shot embedded in his hands.

Julie turned and screamed as she saw Naughton standing there with the gun. It was pretty convincing.

Naughton then fled as Mohinder Cheema lay groaning on the floor. Julie rushed to her husband's side. She looked down at the bloody mess sprawled on the ground and saw that he was still very much alive, despite the cold-blooded attack.

She tried not to look too disappointed. She wondered if maybe the shots would have their desired effect if she just left him there bleeding for a few minutes. She looked outside at Naughton as he made off into the distance and then started crying.

'Oh my God! Mohinder! Oh my God!'

It was an Oscar-winning performance. Two of his children rushed down the stairs from the flat above to help. Meanwhile Julie Cheema ever so slowly called the ambulance service. She did not want them to be too fast, just in case the delay was long enough for her husband to bleed to death. Mohinder Cheema miraculously survived that attack. As Julie held her husband's hand in the ambulance while it rushed to a nearby hospital, she must have been praying he would die. The ambulance crew looked on, in sympathy with the victim's wife. The wives were usually the ones who did most of the suffering. But in the case of Julie Cheema, grieving was just an act of deceit.

She had a horrible feeling that her husband was

going to survive – and that would mean starting her plans all over again. This time they must not fail. Her tears were filled with disappointment, not fear. She had willed him to die but he clearly would not go that easily.

The shooting of Mohinder Cheema created quite a stir in the newspapers that week. The so-called expert crime reporters of the national press were running serious in-depth pieces on the Asian mafia-style gangs that were believed to have gunned down the off-licence owner because he refused to pay protection money.

Reports that the gunman was Asian-looking just helped add fuel to the fire. Neighbours in Cromwell Road were said to be in deep shock about the shooting. Respectable Indian and Pakistani shopkeepers spoke in great detail about their run-ins with these notorious gangs.

Even Julie Cheema voiced her determination not to bow down to these hoods who had so nearly taken away the life of her dearly beloved husband.

'I haven't paid and I won't pay. I work seven days a week and I won't hand over any of my hard-earned money.'

The headline in the Daily Mail that day was:

CORNER SHOP WIFE DEFIES THE MOBSTERS.

Yet, in a bizarre sort of way, Julie Cheema was telling the truth. However, it was her husband whom she suspected of trying to take what was rightfully hers.

Meanwhile, in Charing Cross Hospital, Mohinder Cheema underwent emergency surgery that was simply postponing the death sentence that had already been passed on him.

He had one of his kidneys removed and one of his fingers amputated. He was hailed as a hero in the local press. In fact, the whole incident had some great benefits for Mohinder Cheema. He had become a bit of a local celebrity in his battle to stave off the brutal hitmen from the Asian racketeers.

The millionaire businessman was so convinced by all the publicity that he even hired a team of bodyguards to protect him when he was released from hospital. He was worried about his wife's safety back at the off-licence as well. He even told her to be very careful if she worked there alone. Julie Cheema smiled at him and told him not to worry. She knew full well the gangs were but a figment of his imagination. But she couldn't help chuckling to herself when she realised she had sparked off a feeling of fear in the Asian community. Other killings and shootings of shopkeepers throughout West London were being linked to the Mohinder Cheema case. If only they had known the truth from the outset.

Back in Hounslow, Julie Cheema was determined to make sure her husband was not so lucky a second time around. She was naturally concerned about his plans to hire bodyguards, as she knew it would make her job far more difficult.

Within days of that first shooting, she was scheming and plotting with Neil Marklew, who was still the key player in her plans. But this time, they had a distinct advantage because Mohinder Cheema was absent from the family home.

'This time, you better make sure he dies.'

Julie Cheema could be fairly cold when she wanted to be. She was annoyed with her sweetheart's pal for failing to kill her husband first time around. But she felt an even stronger affinity towards Neil. As they discussed how to make sure the plan really did work, she stroked his youthful face and leant over and kissed him full on the lips. When his tongue began probing her mouth in return, she knew that he would do anything for her.

'It has to be as soon as he gets home. I don't want any of those bodyguards getting in the way.'

Never in a thousand dreams did Neil really expect to go to bed with Julie Cheema. She seemed so much older, so much more mature. He just could not imagine that their friendship would really blossom into all-out sex. But, as Mohinder Cheema lay close to death in hospital, Julie found she could no longer resist the temptation to bed her young friend.

In truth, she had craved his body since the first day they met, but she never had the opportunity to actually seal their lust for one another. But now, with her hubby out of the way, she had the perfect opportunity.

Neil Marklew was delighted that he was being taught some bedroom tricks by Julie. She was so much more experienced than anyone he had ever slept with before. He was perfectly happy to just lie back and let her take control.

As she straddled his body in her bedroom, she realised that he would do anything she commanded.

'You promise he won't miss this time?'

Neil Marklew's mind was on other things when his mature lover suddenly switched the conversation back to the inevitable – her husband.

'Of course I do. I promise you it will be done.'

Julie Cheema continued having sex with her teenage lover and even allowed herself the luxury of a climax for the first time in years. She was really looking forward to the day when she could call all those businesses her own. That would teach her husband to try and cut her out of his will.

But first they had to wait for him to get out of hospital. For six long weeks, Julie Cheema continued her Academy Award-winning performances so as to convince her husband's family and the police that she had nothing whatsoever to do with the vicious attack on her husband.

She even went through the charade of visiting him in hospital. Taking him flowers and fruit as he lay there linked up to heart monitors and drips. She must have been sorely tempted to pull them out of their sockets and just walk calmly away from that room. But Julie knew that all fingers would point at her. No, she had the perfect cover of the Asian gangs out to kill her defiant husband. It was obvious that they would come after him again.

Julie Cheema was genuinely delighted when doctors told her that her husband could go home. It was October 3, 1990 – just six weeks after that first attack. Her happiness was sparked not by her husband's speedy recovery but by the expectation that soon he would be gone for ever. There was no time to waste, as the bodyguards he had hired would be in place the following day.

As she drove him back through West London to his pride and joy – that off-licence in Cromwell Road, Hounslow – she felt the twinge of nervous excitement building up inside. She kept telling him how glad she was that he had been released from hospital. How relieved she was that he had decided to hire minders. Mohinder Cheema looked at his wife in admiration. She really was bearing up to all the stresses and strains very well.

The journey back to their home took no more than forty-five minutes and, just as she knew he would, Mohinder Cheema insisted on taking a look around his off-licence before going off to bed to recuperate. As he walked around the shelves, still in his dressing gown and slippers, inspecting the stock, she realised why she was so glad he was about to be killed. He really was a fussy old man. He did not even trust her enough to let her carry on running the business without interfering. He wanted to know why they were short on stocks of certain brands of wine. She answered him charmingly. Her happiness was hard to contain because she knew that it would not be long now.

When she turned and saw the familiar figure of Robert Naughton approaching the shop, she slipped quietly behind the counter and waited impatiently. Come on. Come on. Let's just get it over and done with.

Just like before, Mohinder Cheema did not notice Naughton until it was too late. This time, he turned towards the gunman and then looked over at his wife standing silently nearby. Mohinder Cheema knew at that moment that she must have been behind it. He could tell from that nervous expression on her lips as he turned to stare death in the face.

Robert Naughton blasted both shots right at his head this time. Basically, he could not fail. Mohinder Cheema's 18-year-old son Sunil – who had just walked into the shop – only realised what was happening when it was too late. If he had turned and seen it coming a few moments earlier, he might have seen that look on his stepmother's face.

The shots hit Mohinder in the back of the head and the neck. There was no way he could survive them this time. He was dead as soon as he hit the floor.

As his son rushed next door to a neighbour to

raise the alarm, Julie Cheema leant down and looked over her husband's injured body for the second time in less than two months. But she could tell immediately that her lover and his friend had succeeded. A warm smile came to her lips and she stood up and walked towards the front of the shop, trying hard to force a sob and a tear to well up in her eyes.

Mohinder Cheema lay there in a pool of blood, still wearing the Charing Cross Hospital dressing-gown he had been wearing when he arrived at the shop just fifteen minutes earlier.

Julie Cheerna was found guilty of murder and attempted murder when she appeared in front of a jury at the Old Bailey in July, 1991. Her lover Neil Marklew and his friend Robert Naughton admitted murder and attempted murder. All three were given life sentences.

Detectives admitted that if it had not been for the testimony of Neil Marklew, Mrs Cheema might never have been arrested.

Her son Kismat, aged 18, was given three months' youth custody for conspiring to murder Mohinder Cheema.

The Toon Case

Miguel Bravo was hard-working, mild and very overweight. He was shy, the sort of guy who would look at the floor when you talked to him. His wife Lucia matched him nearly pound for pound. She was not shy.

Lucia – who was sixteen years his senior – was considered an extremely possessive wife by most of 38-year-old Miguel's relatives. Many friends of the couple believed he was actually terrified of his strong-willed wife.

Miguel earned a lowly $16,000 from his job in a glass factory near the couple's home in Los Angeles and Lucia always insisted he should hand over his entire weekly wage packet. She rarely offered him any of his hard-earned money back, not even the price of a beer.

After Miguel and Lucia married, his relatives warned him that the relationship was sure to end disastrously. They believed she was a bad woman who had an unhealthy influence on her husband.

By 1985, Lucia Bravo was also spending her husband's money on regular, unexplained visits out of Los Angeles. Miguel never once demanded an explanation from his wife; he just wasn't that kind of guy. If she needed to go away now and again then so be it. In any case, he was a bit scared to ask her because he knew she would get very angry with him.

The Bravo family had other mounting problems at that time. They were deeply in debt after investing heavily in buying a number of properties locally. By 1988, they faced a flurry of foreclosure notices and unpaid utility bills.

One night, after one too many arguments, Miguel surprised even himself with his courage in asking Lucia for a divorce. She was stunned. How dare he ask her for a divorce, she thought to herself I will never allow it to happen.

However, Miguel was deadly serious. He had thought long and hard about it and come to the conclusion that Lucia would be better off without him. This wasn't a matter of a husband wanting to run away from his wife to marry some new, young floozie. Miguel genuinely believed he would be doing her a favour by splitting up.

Lucia definitely did not appreciate the finer reasons for her husband's request for a divorce. She looked at it in terms of pride and her Guatemalan background would never permit such a thing to happen. The fact that she was enjoying an extra-marital affair was irrelevant. Men in her home country did it all the time. Why shouldn't she have some fun?

However, Miguel was adamant. A few days after requesting the divorce he moved out of the family's modest single-storey home despite a dire warning from Lucia: 'You are shaming me. I will not let you divorce me, ever.'

Just a few weeks later, the house was raided by burglars who stole everything of value owned by the family. When Miguel popped round to pick up some clothes, he was shocked to find that many of his most prized possessions had gone.

Shortly after that, someone set fire to his car when it was parked outside the cheap motel where he was staying. The police were called but there were no witnesses. Unfortunately, Miguel was not insured.

Then, on 18 November 1988, as the day shift began at the glass factory where Miguel still worked, a white Ford Falcon made a U-turn and parked across the street. At five minutes before six, Miguel emerged and crossed the dimly-lit street. Suddenly, three shots rang out and Miguel crumpled to the ground. A bullet had lodged itself in his jaw and knocked out half of his front teeth. No one got a good look at his assailants or even managed to get the registration number of the car which sped away moments after the attack.

Three days later, Lucia Bravo, then aged 52, visited the Los Angeles Police Department's Wilshire Division, which was then handling the case, to report that she suspected her husband's assailants were one of several moneylenders to whom she and Miguel owed money.

When police visited these moneylenders, they categorically denied all involvement and within three months of the attack on Miguel, the entire investigation had ground to an inactive halt.

Although Miguel eventually recovered from his injuries, doctors said the bullet would have to remain in his jaw for the rest of his life. Lucia was pleasantly surprised when Miguel announced that he was moving into an apartment near their home. She believed that she could still save the marriage, even though her illicit sex sessions with her secret lover continued.

A few days later Miguel narrowly escaped serious injury, or death, when someone else took a pot shot at him outside his new apartment. Three months after that came a third attempt on Miguel's life, when someone else blasted at him in the street, narrowly missing him and his car. Somebody clearly wanted Miguel dead.

A short time later, Miguel was bent over checking the oil level in his car when a fusillade of bullets zinged over his head, missing him by just a hair. A short while after that, a car tried to force him off a motorway while on a trip to Bakersfield, one hundred miles north of Los Angeles.

Miguel was genuinely, and perfectly understandably, fearful for his life by this stage. He knew that someone was out to kill him and he started to tell friends and family that he thought it was only a matter of time before they got him. Miguel began moving around the city, living sometimes with friends, sometimes even in his van.

When Miguel's sister Rosa suggested that Lucia might be behind the murder attempts, he refused to believe that his wife was capable of such a thing. Miguel was so determined not to believe what his sister was saying that he yelled at her: 'Tiene embrujada!' (You are a witch!) He really believed that his sister was bewitched and determined to poison the good name of his estranged wife.

Then, on 24 September 1990, a pipe bomb exploded under Miguel's Thunderbird. Detectives called to the scene were intrigued because there are very few such attacks in terrorist-free Los Angeles. Detective Lawrence Gaffatt was particularly fascinated after he encountered the terrified Miguel Bravo, who miraculously survived the blast despite injuries to his buttocks and groin.

The case became known at the LAPD as the 'toon case after the tough-to-kill cartoon characters. It was almost as if Miguel was as indestructible as Tom the cat. However, this was far from a laughing matter.

Detective Garratt found himself drawn to the case because so many aspects of it just did not add up. He knew instinctively that someone close to Miguel had to be behind the attacks. But what was the purpose of them? The Bravos had denied to Garratt that they had any insurance and he had no legitimate way of checking whether they were telling the truth.

Meanwhile, Miguel Bravo was becoming extremely depressed. He told his sister that he felt his days were definitely numbered. She urged him not to remain in Los Angeles, but Miguel's life revolved around the city and he felt it was his home. In June 1991, he visited his brother and made an off hand remark about planning to drive up to Bakersfield to pick up a car part.

On 26 June, a security guard found Miguel Bravo's body on a dusty piece of ground next to a cotton field canal, just off the old California 99 Highway. Miguel's wallet was still in his pocket, untouched. Kern County Sheriff's detective John Soliz was puzzled by the sobbing of Miguel's widow when he broke the news to her; he could not see a single tear.

Within hours of hearing of her husband's murder, Lucia Bravo was tactlessly suggesting to Miguel's relatives that they should purchase the cheapest coffin available for him. She even arrived late at the funeral when it was held a few days later in Central Los Angeles.

Five months later, an insurance investigator contacted Detective Garratt at the LAPD to verify that Miguel had been murdered, as his wife had just filed a massive insurance claim against his death. Then Garratt got another call about a policy Lucia had taken out, and another and another. In all, a total of five separate policies were taken out during a fifteen-month period before Miguel's death. They all listed Lucia as the main beneficiary.

Confronted by investigators, Lucia at first denied that she had even known of the insurance policies. Then she claimed that Miguel had insisted they keep them all secret. A grand jury subpoena of the Bravos' financial records showed that Lucia Bravo was inexplicably paying premium after premium even while banks were foreclosing on their properties.

Finally, after piecing together a paper trail that took more than two years to compile, authorities arrested Lucia Bravo in Arizona where her son said she had moved to escape threats from her late husband's relatives.

In 1995 Lucia Bravo stood trial and was found guilty and received a life sentence.

Sisters of Mercy

The screams were blood curdling. Ear-piercing yells of pain. Long screeches that echoed into the night.

Then silence. A couple of minutes of blissful silence. Then, another scream. This time even more horrendous. Even more high pitched. Even more agonising.

Five-year-old Charlene Maw and her sister Annette, seven, were lying in their tiny beds too terrified to move.

When they heard their mother let out another anguished cry, they trembled with fear. Too scared to say anything in case he picked on them next.

Then, once more, there was an eery silence from the kitchen downstairs.

The two sisters hoped and prayed that the beating had finished. That their bullying father had ended his drunken frenzy. They looked at each other across the room, praying that he had given her some respite from the vicious attack.

Maybe he had beaten her so badly she lay unconscious? Possibly even close to death?

The inner feelings of these two little girls were already damaged beyond repair.

On that terrible evening, the quiet that then descended on the ordinary looking semi-detached home in the Yorkshire town of Bradford seemed to indicate the worst was over.

The little girls tried to get back to sleep in preparation for the full day of school that lay just a few hours ahead.

Tears streaked down their cheeks as they listened to the unmistakable sound of footsteps clumping up the stairs.

Their father was stumbling drunkenly to their bedroom one clumsy step at a time. Half way up he tripped and cursed the carpenter who had built the damn thing.

Charlene and Annette were shaking in their beds – terrified that his footsteps would stop outside their room.

The door burst open and 50-year-old Thomas Maw appeared – an ominous shadow in the doorway. Just a black shape filling the entire entrance. The stale stench of cider filled the air as he stood swaying from side to side.

The girls pretended to be asleep. Their faces screwed up tightly in case he made eye-contact. They could feel his eyes boring down on them. Examining their faces for any clues to whether they were actually awake.

Even through his drunken stupor, Thomas Maw knew his young daughters were pretending to be asleep. A lip-curling smile crawled up one side of his face. Just a hint of his back teeth caught the light shining from the hallway.

The first to feel the back of his hand was Annette. He slapped her across the face.

'Get up. Get up you little bitch. I want to show you something.'

Annette could see the hatred in his bloodshot eyes. It scared her. She was confused. Too upset to fight back. Too scared to say 'No'. As he grabbed her nighty, she felt like a rag doll in giant hands. She could feel the force of his grip as he made her stand to attention. She trembled with cold and fear.

Next came Charlene. Having seen her father assault her sister, she was so scared that she got out of bed immediately. Desperate to avoid the sort of brutal back handers she had just watched Annette suffer.

Little brother Bryn, aged three, was the only one who had been genuinely asleep. But then he was a boy and boys do not always feel the full wrath of their father's anger.

'Get downstairs. Now!'

Maw was slurring his words, spittle flying from his mouth. He kept snorting through his nose. Lost for breath and wheezing one moment, shouting and cursing the next. But the message was loud and clear.

'Get down there NOW!'

Annette and Charlene were petrified. Perhaps he had killed their mother and wanted to show them the body as a warning to them all to behave?

The two little girls knew one thing though – they had to get down to that kitchen as fast as possible if they were going to save their mother's life. He would give her another beating if they did not obey. He was always blaming her for their behaviour.

All three little children rushed down the stairway, desperate to see if their mother was alright. Inside the tiny kitchen, pots and pans were scattered everywhere amongst fragments of broken plates on the linoleum floor. And there on the floor, amongst the debris, was Beryl Maw. A clump of her hair was hanging from her scalp where he had tried to tear it off. Her face was red down one side. But she was conscious. Desperately trying to compose herself so that the children would not see what an awful beating he had inflicted on her.

She could take the punches and the scratches, but when he tried to rip out her hair by its roots, that really drove home the message that she had married a monster. Yet in his more sober moments, Maw would confess that he was jealous of her curly brown locks. It seemed so bizarre for a husband to be envious of his wife's hair. But he actually used to make her keep it short and dyed black. One day she asked him why.

He just screwed up his eyes in fury and shouted: 'It's so bloody curly. I wish I had hair like you.' For the first time in more than 20 years of marriage, Beryl had discovered what drove her husband into blazing temper tantrums – her hair. It was as frightening as it was ludicrous.

Back in that wrecked kitchen that evening, Mrs Maw was just thankful to be alive. She had glimpsed the other side and didn't want to go there yet.

Annette and Charlene rushed to her and hugged her protectively. They were relieved to see she was still conscious, despite being black and blue from her husband's attack.

They held her tightly. But it was difficult for her to return their affection. Just to squeeze her arms around the girls was agony. Everything ached so much. But it was her head that really hurt. It throbbed from ear to ear. It was unbearable. The pain seared left to right, right to left, increasing every time she made any slight movement. When she rubbed her scalp with her hand she felt the gaping wounds where he had ripped whole clumps of hair out by the roots.

Frightened Bryn cowered in the corner of the tiny kitchen. Bemused. Puzzled. He didn't understand. It was one in the morning. Why had they been made to go downstairs in the middle of the night? Were they going some place? He just wanted to go back to his teddy bears and bed. He was confused. But even he could feel the tight atmosphere – it was fused with hatred.

And Thomas Maw certainly knew what it was all about. That was why he had forced his young family to come downstairs. He looked into the eyes of his two daughters. They looked away the moment they caught his glance. Scared. Appalled by his behaviour. Disgusted at what had happened. How could he do such a thing?

They tried to hug their mother even tighter. But he saw it as an act of defiance that could not go unpunished. Their look of contempt for him was enough to ignite a further onslaught.

The look reminded him of his wife. The woman he had taken solemn vows with twenty years earlier. The same woman he had just spent the previous two hours trying to beat to a pulp.

Without warning, he grabbed Beryl by the hair and pulled her towards him. The children grimaced with horror. He was starting up all over again.

They couldn't stand to look. But they felt that if they turned away he would beat her even more viciously. He wanted them to watch. If they did not, he might finish her off forever.

Charlene couldn't take much more. She could not bear the expression on her mother's face. Alternating from a grimace of excruciating agony to a dull, blank, far-away stare.

She tried to push him away from her mother. He simply swiped her to the floor and warned the other two: 'You're next if you're not careful.'

Then, as if he were a teacher demonstrating to a classroom of pupils, he said: 'This is what I do when your mother disobeys me and this is what I'll do to you.'

The children winced as yet more handfuls of hair were torn from their mother's scalp. He was pulling with such ferocity that her head was being jerked from side to side. As the hair ripped out there was an awful noise, like splitting cardboard.

"Stop Dad. Stop. Please stop," the girls begged their father. But he was not interested in their pleas. He wanted to make them suffer. Teach them all a lesson – a lesson in obedience.

Then he held his wife's hair with one hand while he smashed her face on the edge of the kitchen sink with the other. Her teeth crunched as they connected with the metal.

The children were screaming now, but he ignored them. Determined to wreak an awful revenge upon the woman he was supposed to adore and cherish.

By the time her head crashed on the sink for the fourth time, Beryl Maw was on the verge of a blackout. She could just make out her three children, standing transfixed by this awful picture of domestic horror.

The pain of watching their faces as he continued unabated, was almost as bad as the physical agony she was enduring. Just to see them being forced to witness this attack was punishment in itself.

She strained to keep her eyes open. Afraid of what he might do to them once she was gone.

Then she lost consciousness.

Thomas Maw had beaten his wife senseless. The provocation? Smiling at him in an off guard moment a few hours earlier.

It was the first time Charlene and her sister Annette had seen their father's brutality – but it was an image that would keep coming back to them over and over again as the years went by.

For once in his life, Thomas Maw was behaving like the true gentleman his wife Beryl had fallen in love with and married nearly twenty years earlier.

They had been out for a meal in an expensive restaurant and she actually felt that perhaps there was some future for them together.

Mrs Maw had endured years of beatings from her husband but somehow never felt the courage to get up and leave it all behind.

There were always so many other considerations. The children. The house. All the things that keep families together through thick and thin.

Now she felt that perhaps it had all been worthwhile. He was making such an effort tonight. He seemed to want to make amends. To win back her love after years of torment. To show that he really cared. But Mrs Maw still had a nagging doubt in the back of her mind.

She had always promised herself she would get up and leave him once the children were old enough to cope. Now, here he was turning on the old charm. The charm that he had used so effectively when they had first met at a dance so long ago. He was a suave airman who had swept her off her 17-year-old feet.

They were married just a few weeks later.

But the Thomas Maw she knew then was unrecognisable now.

Even on their wedding anniversary he had managed to get drunk. But at least he was being nice to her. It made a change.

As they drove home from the restaurant she wondered if he really was going to turn over a new leaf. Perhaps he could change back into the man he had once been.

Beryl felt almost relaxed in his company that evening. It was the first time in years she had felt that way.

Thomas Maw was feeling happy too. But his mind was on things other than his marriage as he drove along the busy streets in the town's liveliest late night area.

Mrs Maw then noticed the car was slowing down by the kerbside. She was puzzled. What was wrong? Was the car about to breakdown? She looked over at her husband for a reaction. He didn't even acknowledge her.

No. Thomas Maw had spotted two prostitutes cruising along an empty pavement. His wife may have been sitting right next to him, but he wanted those women. It didn't matter what she thought. She could go to hell if she didn't like it.

He slowed down to proposition them. Beryl Maw could not believe her eyes as her husband rolled down the window and whistled the girls across to him.

'How much?' He asked in a nonchalant manner. The women were almost as surprised as Mrs Maw by his behaviour. After all, how many men stop to pick up a street walker with their wives sitting next to them?

One of them leant over to talk to Maw.

'How dare you.' Beryl was indignant with rage. How could he do this after they had enjoyed such a great night together.

The prostitutes took a step back. They sensed an explosion was about to occur. They even had a sympathetic look on their faces. As if to say: 'How could this man be such a filthy pig?'

Thomas Maw did not see it that way. Women existed to be used and abused. What right had his own wife to stop him picking up a street walker?

He was infuriated that the two women were now walking away. Enraged that his wife had the nerve to decide whether he should pay two compete strangers for sex.

Maw aimed his fist straight at his wife's face. Her

nose exploded in a shower of blood. He followed through with other blows to the body.

By the time they arrived home, Beryl Maw had suffered two black eyes, a broken tooth and bruised ribs. Thomas Maw would never change his ways.

'That bloody rabbit has to go.' Thomas Maw was drunk yet again. This time he was throwing his verbal abuse in the direction of Charlene and Annette's pet rabbit. He was furious they had built a hutch for the animal without asking his permission first.

The children grabbed the rabbit out of the hutch and ran into the house. But Thomas Maw had decided that it had to die. Grabbing a knife from the kitchen he charged after the terrified little girls. They stumbled as they raced up the stairs to their room. The rabbit jumped out of their hands – straight into the path of Mr Maw.

He grabbed the white, furry creature and gleefully stuck the knife into its belly, twisting the blade menacingly just to make certain. He did it right in front of the little girls, relishing their distress.

The rabbit was dead. But Maw had another grisly surprise up his sleeve. Three hours later the family sat down to a lunch of rabbit stew. He made them eat up every mouthful.

Maw's cruelty towards animals knew no bounds. They couldn't answer back, so that made them even better victims. He would take awful delight in gassing mice and flies in the kitchen oven, watching them through the window as they contorted and twisted.

Worse was to come. They listened to him kicking a puppy to death in his bedroom – all because it had urinated in the hallway. Only a few days earlier it had been given to them as a present.

Many other awful incidents followed but Thomas Maw surpassed even his appalling standards when the children found a frog in the garden. Snatching the creature out of Annette's hands, he took it into the kitchen and beckoned the children to follow him. They were scared. They knew he was about to do something horrible. They also knew they would get an awful beating if they did not do as they were told.

In the kitchen, Maw took out a straw and told the children to watch carefully. They were puzzled. He never bothered to show them interesting tricks normally. In fact, he hardly ever even acknowledged their existance, calling them 'stupid bastards' most of the time.

But, looking at his smiley, cheery face, they presumed he was about to act like a real father and play a game with them.

Now he had the children's attention, he placed the straw inside the frog's mouth. Still the youngsters were baffled. They could not work out what he was about to do. He was being so friendly towards the frog all the time, stroking it and loving it. They guessed it was going to be something nice and it made them all feel warm and excited inside.

Maw leant down and put the other end of the straw

to his lips. His eyes looked up at the children just to make sure they were watching.

They saw the glint then. The expectant look. But they just thought he wanted to make sure they did not miss the trick.

They watched him take a deep breath inwards. Then he blew with all his might. The tiny frog ballooned up, getting bigger and bigger. It began to look like a toy. Not a real, living creature.

Little Bryn began to laugh. Charlene and Annette did not laugh. They knew by now that what their father was doing was cruel and nasty – the work of a madman.

Suddenly the frog exploded like a balloon that's been fed too much air. Bits of its green scaly body flew across the kitchen, hitting the children with a wet sting. They cried with horror, unable to understand what had driven their father to do such an evil thing.

The girls ran to their room and refused to come down for days. Beryl Maw now knew beyond doubt that she was married to a monster.

On 27th March, 1989, Thomas Maw poured himself the first of ten pints of cider he was to consume that evening. Sitting in the front room of his home in Ranelagh Avenue, Bradford, he supped thirstily at the pint glass in his hand. He was feeling tense as usual and desperately wanted to feel the rush of alcohol to his brain.

In a place like Bradford, most men go to the pub for a drink. But Maw's ferocious temper had got him banned from every single one in the area. Those landlords had taken the sort of measures Mrs Maw should have taken years earlier.

The rest of his family were nowhere to be seen. They knew better than to hang about when Maw decided to go on a drinking spree. No one except his ever loyal wife would even talk to Maw by now. It had just got too much for the rest of the family. Yet somehow, through all the punches and the slaps, Beryl still loved and adored her beast of a husband. She had already endured so much battering that the pain no longer mattered.

'It was fear and helplessness. I had lost sight of who I was,' she said later.

Then there were his terror tactics – deliberately intended to warn her who was in control. One night she remembered him saying: 'Leave me and one dark night I'll find you and that will be it.'

Mrs Maw believed his every word.

But that night, she sat willingly in the living room with her husband as he downed pint after pint. Her daughters kept warning her to keep away from him.

'He's the devil in disguise mum.'

Annette was by now an attractive 21-year-old and Charlene fast catching up at 18. They had their own lives to lead. But they always swore they would not leave her to his mercy. That monster would have to leave the house first.

Beryl made polite, nervous small talk with her husband about the weather and the day's news. It was hardly the level of conversation that a married couple should enjoy. More like a meeting between two complete strangers. But she was so anxious to please – even after the awful life she had suffered.

The tense atmosphere took care of that. All the time there was this overwhelming awkwardness. As the minutes passed, she could feel him building up. Getting more and more angry within himself. It was only a matter of time.

But still Mrs Maw sat there, praying and hoping that perhaps they could enjoy a night together. Just the two of them relaxing in the comfort of their own home.

It was something her two daughters would never understand. Why had she let him make her suffer so much? The answer probably lay with them. They were the reason she carried on.

'What do you think of this Margaret Thatcher?' asked Mr Maw. But before his wife had a chance to answer he followed up.

'Bloody woman isn't she?'

Maw was spoiling for a fight yet again.

In the kitchen Charlene and Annette could hear the sound of raised voices. They knew it was the first sign of trouble.

Weeks earlier they had promised each other they would not allow his beatings to continue.

'We have got to do something – before it's too late,' said Annette at the time.

Now they had to turn those words into action.

'I've had enough. I'm going in there to tell him what I think of him.'

Annette had cracked. She could take no more. In recent years, he had started taking it out on her as well as their mother.

She was haunted by all the awful incidents. Like the time she had spent five hours doing a drawing for her 'O' level preparations and he ripped it up into tiny pieces – just because she had smiled at him.

He would beat her regularly calling her 'stupid' and 'thick'.

Now he was about to beat her mother yet again. She could not take it anymore. She had to act – now.

Annette wanted to protect her mother. The only way was to confront the beast.

Ironically, as Annette charged through the corridor towards the front room, she strongly resembled her father. Maybe it was the way she was walking, but she reminded her sister of the way their father looked at his worst.

Charlene had no option but to follow her through the house to the front room. She pleaded with Annette to calm down. She genuinely feared their father could turn so nasty it would prove deadly one day. That day might have come.

The two girls stormed in. The diversion at least gave their mother some respite. An interlude in the cruel catalogue of violence. Maw vented his anger in the girls' direction, starting with Charlene.

'Just get out of here, you useless fucking bitch.'Charlene was not going to just soak up the abuse. The time had come. Her mother had put up with too much for too long.

'You're scum,' she shouted back.

Maw visibly boiled with anger at that reply. He saw himself as the man of the household. And here was his own daughter calling him names.

For a split second he looked menacingly at both defiant girls standing before him.

'I am not going to take this,' he screamed.

Punches rained down on the back of Charlene's head. She had become the first one to feel the full force of his temper.

Maw's eyes were twisted up as he concentrated on thumping her as hard as he could. Harder and harder. He kept crashing his massive fists down on her neck bone. He wanted to crush her body, bludgeon her spirit until it caved in.

Even though they had all been expecting it, it took them all slightly by surprise. He had done it so many times before but on this occasion it seemed worse than ever.

He was delirious with anger.

Then Annette joined in.

She tried to jump on her father's back to stop him throwing his punches. It was an impossible task.

'Stop you bastard. Stop.' The screaming was even louder than before. They were fighting back this time. They were not going to let him get away with it. They had soaked up enough punishment. Now it was their turn to attack.

Maw relaxed his vicious onslaught for a moment.

Regathering his energy before starting all over again.

Charlene now had the opportunity to grab her sister by the hand and run to the shelter of their bedroom. It had been the only place throughout their childhood where he had not dared to inflict punishment.

Now they prayed he would respect their sanctuary.

As they dashed through the house, Charlene could feel the throbbing on her injured neck. Behind them they heard the drunken insults of their father. He was coming after them. He wanted to finish them off for good.

It was like a scene from the worst type of horror movie. He was chasing them. Every moment getting closer and closer.

But this was real life.

As they scrambled up the stairs, Maw lunged at Annette's ankle. He held on tight. She felt herself lose balance. She could not control it. She was falling backwards into his vice-like grasp. Charlene grabbed her arm and a human tug of war was waged on the stairway.

Maw pulled with all his might. Suddenly he lost balance and his daughter aimed a sharp kick to his face She was free momentarily. But the chase was still on.

The stair carpet came loose and he lost his footing

as the girls looked behind them. They were relieved to have escaped his grasp but they knew he would still come after them.

Somehow, he regained his footing and climbed the stairs three at a time. His anger seemed to be giving him fresh impetus in the race to the bedroom.

As Charlene turned to slam the door shut, she felt his weight against the door, forcing it open again. She tried with all her might to keep closing it. But the sheer strength of her father was too much.

For a few desperate seconds they pulled and pushed the door each way until he finally burst through.

Now he was in their room. They both had their backs to the paint peeled walls. Terrified of what was about to happen.

'Dad. Let's talk about this.' Charlene was trying to calm him down. A peaceful approach might work. He seemed to hesitate for a moment, responding to his daughter's appeal.

Maybe he could see how dreadful he had been?

Then an umbrella came crashing down towards his head.

Annette saw it now as all out war – and this was no time to start waving the white flag.

Just as as the brolly was about to hit dead centre on his crown, Maw grabbed at it and pulled it out of her grasp.

He was in control once more. He had the upper hand and now he was going to teach those daughters of his a lesson they would never forget.

Grabbing Annette by the wrist, he threw a volley of punches at her. Once again, he aimed at the back of the neck. A favourite spot for family battering.

Perhaps he knew the bruises would not show so clearly.

Then Mrs Maw appeared at the door. The sight of her husband trying to kill their eldest daughter had inspired her to stoop to his level. She was armed with a huge mirror – ready to use at the earliest opportunity.

She pulled him to the floor and smashed the mirror over his head. The pieces scattered around the room. Maw lay unconscious. The beast had been tamed for a short while.

The three women were drained. Even by their father's appalling standards this was the nearest to death any of them had ever come. For a few seconds none of them said anything as they walked downstairs to recover from their ordeal.

In the kitchen Annette broke the silence.

'Let's kill him before he kills us.' She was shaking from shock. Mrs Maw felt the same way. She nodded in agreement. But Charlene was horrified.

'Don't be so bloody stupid. Let's just leave him where he is and call the police.' She wanted justice, not bloody retribution.

The other two women stopped and thought for a second. They knew in their heart of hearts that Charlene was right, but events clouded their judgement. All they could think about were the beatings, the insults and the terror. Year in, year out at the hands of a sick monster who deserved no mercy. Now they had a chance to do something about it. A chance to avenge incidents like the time he threatened to gas his own children when they annoyed him.

'The Gestapo had it about right. I just wish I had been Himmler then I could have had you lot put down at birth.'

Thomas Maw was no joker. He had looked menacingly into his children's eyes as they all sat down one meal time. He had meant it.

However terrible he had been though, murder, whatever the motives, was wrong. Pure and simple. They knew that. They should look at the situation objectively. Recognise the symptoms and deal with them.

But human emotions are not that easy to contain.

The police should have been called there and then. But something held them back. They wanted to deal with him in their own way. Turn the tables on him. Even if they did call the police, it required a real effort because they had no telephone. It made it more difficult to reach the obvious, sensible decision.

Nevertheless they had to decide what to do before he regained consciousness.

'Go next door and call the police. We've got to get him out of this house.' Both Annette and her mother had come round and seen sense.

The temptation to take the law into their own hands had passed. It would have seemed 'just' to cause him some pain – just as he had done to them for so long. But, underneath it all, they knew the police were the only answer. They could deal with him. Hopefully, the courts would put him away for a very long time.

Charlene was relieved. For a few desperate minutes she had seemed to be the only person in that house who wanted to take the correct course of action. The only way of dealing with a fascist is to become a fascist – unless sense prevails. Finally it had.

Charlene went to put on a coat. She had to hurry.

Upstairs, Maw was stirring.

A hand grabbed Annette around the throat. She hadn't seen it coming.

Maw was going to finish his private war with his own family. His wife and daughters might have decided to treat him like a human being, but he was not going to do them that service in return.

Annette was gasping for breath. He was smiling gleefully at his other daughter and her mother as he I held Annette by the throat.

Maybe he had heard about their plans to murder him? Perhaps he had decided to kill them before they managed to do away with him? One thing was for certain. Maw was now trying his hardest to murder Annette.

'Get a knife.' Annette was struggling to spit out the words but Charlene understood what she was saying.

She hesitated, still longing for a peaceful solution Even as their father stood there trying to choke her sister to death, she hoped he would stop and they could sit down and discuss their problems, instead of turning that night into a life or death struggle.

Charlene hesitated … but she knew.

There was no time. She had to get the knife.

'For God's sake … He's killing me!'

Charlene ran to the kitchen and grabbed the nearest knife she could find. She could have picked the huge carving knife on the sideboard, but she chose the small cutlery knife instead.

Annette grabbed it from her and plunged it into Maw's body. She had to be quick. She might not live much longer …

As the blade sank into his stomach, Annette felt her father let go. She thought she had plunged it deep into his body but as he turned it just snapped in two. It did not even penetrate his outer layer of skin.

Now the monster had switched victims and was punching his wife viciously like a prize fighter desperate to gain an instant knock-out.

'A bigger one! Quick!' Annette screamed.

Annette was trying desperately to stop her father from killing her mother. She punched him in the back, but it had little effect. It just drove him on to further violence. Charlene went back into the kitchen once more. This time she got the carving knife that would finish off the job.

Annette snatched the knife away from her younger sister like a heroin user grabbing at her fix. But she was more desperate than any drug addict. She had to kill him before he struck first.

She plunged the seven inch blade into his neck, severing the jugular vein in one quick motion. But he still kept punching, despite blood gushing from the wound all over his wife and daughter. So Annette continued to stab at the neck with all the strength she could muster. Within seconds the monster had crumpled in a heap on the floor.

At last the pain and suffering would be no more.

Annette and Charlene Maw were each jailed for three years when they admitted killing Thomas Maw, before a judge at Leeds Crown Court on 17th Nov, 1980. They were originally charged with murder but this was reduced to manslaughter.

A later appeal against their sentence saw Charlene's term cut by six months. Annette's appeal was dismissed.

Charlene was said to have 'played a lesser part' in the killing, according to the appeal court judge, Lord Lane.

He said Annette was the probable organiser of the offence. At the time of their original sentencing, Judge Mr Justice Smith acknowledged that the sisters had been provoked and that their life was 'a sad history'. But he also added, 'It is also a very sad duty I have to perform because you deliberately and unlawfully stabbed and killed him'.

Fistful of Dollars

Cancun, Mexico, is one of those beachside paradises that most people can only dream about – miles and miles of pure white sand overlooking the Gulf of Mexico. A picturesque whitewashed town with a handful of luxurious hotels for wealthy American tourists, plus a scattering of bars and restaurants attractively decorated and designed to guarantee hundreds of thousands of visitors each year.

Mary Ellen Samuels from California had always

wanted to go south of the border. It seemed so exotic on the television and it appeared to be the perfect place to escape from her worries back in California. So it was that attractive brunette Mary Ellen found herself on a get-away-from-it all holiday. The perfect picture was made complete by the presence of her young lover, who would provide the sex and cocaine that had been a staple need for Mary Ellen most of her adult life.

Most evenings, she and her lover would enjoy at least two bottles of wine in the hotel restaurant before slipping up to their suite where Mary Ellen knew that some athletic love making was sure to occur.

On one particular night they virtually had sex up against the bedroom door because their lust was proving so insatiable. Mary Ellen was always game to try anything within seconds of wrapping her arms around her young lover. For the first time in years, she felt completely free to do as she pleased. Her boring husband was dead. She no longer had to hide her secret vices from the world.

That evening she opened up a sachet of cocaine and laid out four, fat, two-inch lines of cocaine, then pulled out a handful of twenty-dollar bills before finding the crispest note which she expertly rolled into a makeshift straw before snorting her lines hungrily.

'I got an idea,' said her lover as he snorted the second of his lines. 'Gimme all the cash you got.'

Mary Ellen hesitated for a moment. She had

worked and schemed very hard for her money.

'Come on. I ain't gonna take it. I just wanna show you how to have some fun.'

Then her handsome boyfriend started spreading twenty-dollar bills on top of the bed. Mary Ellen smiled and took a deep, excited breath. Earlier that holiday they had talked of making love in a sea of cash. Now their mutual fantasy was about to come true.

Mary Ellen stripped off her clothes and lay on top of the first layer of notes, then her boyfriend carefully covered her body with the rest of the crispest of the new twenty-dollar bills; their sharp corners enhancing the sensation of literally swimming in money. Mary Ellen could feel the notes cutting slightly into her nipples every time she moved while he continued to lay them all over her. It was a pleasant sensation.

Eventually, she was covered in the money, except for a small gap at the top of her thighs. He looked down at her face. It wore a smug, satisfied expression, then she slowly licked her lips with the tip of her tongue. Her young lover looked on in awe.

'Come on, baby. It's time to show me how much you love me,' exclaimed the sultry, dark-haired, one-time housewife. She edged her legs apart a few inches. 'Come here.'

The woman dubbed by police as the 'Green Widow' was living up to her name. For her bizarre sex romp in a sea of money was just part of her celebration following an enormous insurance payout of half a million dollars after the apparently tragic murder of her Hollywood cameraman husband by a cold-blooded stranger.

A few months earlier, the slaying had struck fear into the suburban communities of the San Fernando Valley area of California, just twenty miles from the sprawling metropolis of Los Angeles. Inside the Hollywood movie community, many were mourning the loss of respected technician Bob Samuels, who had been closely associated with stars like Warren Beatty and Mel Gibson.

Sinking deeper into the mass of green paper, Mary Ellen pulled her young lover on to the bed and proceeded to make hot, passionate love. A luxurious life was, it seemed, sealed for ever.

With her neat hairstyle and fondness for sleek, well-fitting business suits, Mary Ellen Samuels certainly looked the part of a wealthy middle-aged widow, but she had been nursing a secret addiction to sex, drugs, drink and risk-taking for more years than anyone could care to remember.

It later transpired that this forty-five-year-old mother had ordered a hitman to kill her Hollywood cameraman husband – and then murdered the hired assassin once he had gunned down his victim. Soon afterwards she was dubbed the Green Widow after banking a fortune in insurance claims following her husband's death.

'It was a classic story of greed and manipulation

combined with a callous disregard for human life,' said Van Nuys, California prosecuting attorney Jan Maurizi. 'This was a very attractive woman who had an uncanny ability to manipulate people and used her talents to get rich. Just about anybody whose life she touched became a victim. Basically, her husband was worth more to Mary Ellen dead than alive.'

This extraordinary story began on 3 December 1988, when her husband, forty-year-old Robert B. Samuels – who had worked on films like *Lethal Weapon* and *Heaven Can Wait* – was ambushed inside the house the couple had shared until their separation a year earlier.

The 'burglar' shot Samuels in the head with a 16-gauge shotgun. Police were alerted by Mary Ellen and her eighteen-year-old daughter Nicole after they arrived at the house to find her husband's bloodied corpse.

Samuels later boasted to friends: 'I should have won an Academy Award for my acting performance. I was the perfect grieving widow.'

However, detectives were suspicious because there was no apparent sign of a struggle. It also soon became clear that Mary Ellen was a very spoilt wife. She rapidly collected an insurance bonanza of $500,000 and went on a wild spending spree of parties, pals and drugs.

She splashed out $60,000 on a Porsche, rented stretch limos most weekends and even took her toyboy to Mexico to buy a villa in the sun. While on that secret holiday, she posed for photographs lying naked on $20,000 worth of the cash she had just been paid by insurers.

At the time of Samuels's death, detectives did not know that Mary Ellen's hitman, Robert B. Bernstein, had previously failed three times to knock off unsuspecting Bob Samuels.

Once Bernstein had plotted with Mary Ellen to push his car off a cliff and twice they had planned to shoot him after getting him drunk, but each scheme failed at the final hurdle. Finally, Bernstein had to hire another man – who later shot himself – to finish off Bob Samuels.

Explained prosecutor Maurizi: 'She was really pretty pampered by her husband. Her child was in private school. I think she had what the average American would consider the good life. But half of it wasn't going to be good enough for her.'

Also in court, Samuels's former husband Ronnie Lee Jamison conceded that she had been a compulsive liar who gambled and used drugs during their marriage.

Six months after Samuels's slaying, a botany professor on a nature hike found the body of suspected hitman Bernstein, a twenty-seven-year-old reputed cocaine dealer, which had been dumped in a remote canyon in nearby Ventura County.

It later emerged that Mary Ellen had hired two more hitmen to do away with Bernstein because he had started demanding more money and had threatened to go to the police if she did not pay. She paid her replacement hitmen a paltry $5,000 and a packet of drugs.

Stupidly, the merry widow insisted on keeping Bernstein's wallet in her Porche as a souvenir, where police later found it. They also discovered a diary for murder which read in part: 'People are saying I did it. Nailed me for Bob, want me for Jim.

Mary Ellen's defence team even tried to claim that Bernstein – who carried a business card calling himself 'James R. Bernstein, specialist' – was smitten with the Samuels' daughter, Nicole. They insisted he acted on his own when he killed Robert Samuels after Nicole told him that Robert Samuels had raped her when she was just twelve years old.

Other friends and relatives of the couple insisted that Mary Ellen had arranged the killing of her husband in revenge for his sex attacks on her daughter. No one was ever able to establish if her claims were true.

Maurizi dismissed the sexual molestation charges as pure fabrication. Robert Samuels's sister, Susan Conroy, said: 'It's the ultimate betrayal. He isn't here to defend himself. Bob was a hard-working guy and he loved them very much. He would never have done anything to them.'

Paul Edwin Gaul and Darell Ray Edwards – the men who admitted killing original hitman Bernstein – testified against Mary Ellen Samuels after striking a deal with prosecutors who agreed to commute any death sentence against them. They were sentenced before her trial to fifteen years to life for the murder of Bernstein.

The Samuels' marriage originally broke up in 1987 when Mary Ellen moved out, taking the refrigerator and leaving a five-page 'Dear John' letter. She moved to a condominium in nearby Reseda, California. For more than a year, Mr Samuels hoped they might be reconciled.

However, reconciliation was far from Mrs Samuels' mind. One old family friend, Heidi Dougall, recalled: 'She hated him and she wanted him done.'

She even told friends that she had calculated that she would receive only $30,000 in a divorce settlement, as opposed to the $100,000 she knew her husband was worth dead.

Mary Ellen's biggest bone of contention with her husband was over their shared ownership of a sandwich shop in nearby Sherman Oaks. She was also reluctant to wave goodbye to the $1,600 a month in maintenance that she was receiving.

During part of 1988, the vengeful wife once again told friends that she was considering having her husband 'done away with'. Soon she was even approaching her daughter's high-school friends. She insisted that she wanted revenge for her husband's attempts to molest her daughter. In one extraordinary incident, daughter Nicole even turned to a friend for help in the cafeteria. The stunned classmate later gave evidence against Samuels at her trial.

Even though Mary Ellen protested her innocence, the evidence was overwhelming and she was found guilty of two counts of murder, two counts of conspiracy to murder and two counts of solicitation for murder.

'I've never asked for the death penalty for a woman before,' said prosecutor Maurizi, who is still considering filing charges against Mary Ellen's daughter Nicole. 'But these murders were premeditated, six months apart and motivated purely through greed. Mary Ellen Samuels was a housewife who went shopping for something other suburban housewives don't need. She went shopping for killers!'

Maurizi also said to the jury: 'I ask you for a verdict of death for all the selfish and inhumane decisions she made in her life. I ask you, ladies and gentlemen, how many bodies does it take? We're talking about murder for the sake of the almighty dollar.'

On 16 September 1994, Mary Ellen Samuels became only the fifth woman in history to be sentenced to death in California since the state reimposed capital punishment in the late 1970s. She will die in the gas chamber or through a lethal injection.

As juror Karen Hudson explained outside the court following sentencing: 'We wanted to let people know we were sure.'

The Black Widow

Winnacunnet High School was the sort of place educationalists dream about.

Nestling on the edge of the quiet New England town of Hampton, it enjoyed a reputation as one of the finest schools in the North Eastern United States. None of those classic inner city problems of violence and truancy existed here. This was middle America. Simple. No Frills. A pleasant environment where people were at peace with themselves.

The white wood detached houses with their neatly trimmed front lawns that dominated the area, were classic evidence of that harmony. The immaculately clean streets throughout the picture postcard town centre summed up the pride which residents of Hampton had in their town. It was a relatively small, tightly knit community where everyone knew each other. There was a familiarity about the place that made you feel instantly at home.

All in all it represented a fairly large chunk of the American dream. Virtually no crime and even fewer scandals.

And the sons and daughters of Hampton residents were brought up to honour and obey those rules. While many of them were allowed their own car by the age of sixteen, there was a strictly enforced alcohol rule that prevented any person under the age of thirty from buying booze unless they provided an ID card.

Parents were determined to bring their children up in a responsible way. Constantly lecturing them about the evils of drink and drugs. Always preventing them from doing anything wild.

It was the same in the classrooms of Winnacunnet High. That strict moral code was abided by to the letter. And anyone who stepped out of line was severeley punished. But, out of all this discipline, there were, inevitably, the rebels. The youngsters who only wanted to do the opposite of what their family hoped for. The teenagers who saw that all these rules and regulations were made to be broken.

Bill Flynn, Patrick Randall and Vance Lattime were weary of being repressed by their parents. They were sick and tired of conforming. They wanted to be different.

As the three 15-year-olds hung around in the school playground one cold November day, discussing how awful their families were, there seemed to be little in life for them to look forward to. College exams were fast approaching and they were under constant pressure to perform well. To them, learning was not an interesting pastime. It was that common bond of apathy that sealed their friendship. They had all recognised in each other a total disdain for schoolwork. It drew them together.

Each time one of them was in trouble in class, it became a very special mark of distinction. The other two would look on proudly when their friend was punished. They saw it as yet more evidence of why they had to get out of school as quickly as possible – which was quite a problem for the three friends.

The staff at Winnacunnet pushed relentlessly for their pupils to go on to college – no matter what. Academically and sportingly, they were all expected to excel. But Bill, Patrick and Vance had other ideas. In an attempt to separate themselves from the majority of hard working classmates, they even decided to call themselves 'The Three Musketeers'.

'That way people will know we are different,' said Bill. He had become the self-appointed ring leader despite looking even younger than his years.

Basically, Bill, Patrick and Vance were more intrigued by the girls in their grade than the history of art. Their idea of fun was discussing the prowess of their favourite girls – even though they might never have even touched them.

'Hey. Wouldn't you just love to ...' Bill was trying to get a response out of his quieter friend Vance. They were discussing what they would like to do to one particularly sexy looking blonde classmate. She was glancing over in their direction from the other side of the playground. She seemed to be encouraging them. Maybe she could hear what they were saying?

The boys were smirking. Excited at the prospect. They had interpreted the girl's acknowledgement as a certain invitation for sex – even though none of them had uttered more than a few words to her. In truth, she was just flirting in that inimitable way only teenage girls can. Just glancing every so often. Encouraging the boys' adolescent minds at every moment.

The Three Musketeers had another good reason to get out of school at the earliest opportunity. They were all virgins. But they didn't like admitting it to themselves – let alone their pals. They tended to swap imaginary tales of their sexual conquests in the hope it would convince their pals what experienced men they really were.

'Maybe she's just after your body Vance,' said Bill

when he spotted Vance staring wistfully in the direction of that pretty classmate.

From the opposite corner of the playground, another older woman was watching the three boys. But they did not notice.

Class was about to restart – and that meant more mindless learning.

They quickly shared a cigarette butt in the corner of the vast grey concrete covered playground and all agreed there must be more to life than just school. They were all about to find out. A lot sooner than they realised.

The older woman was still watching the threesome. Holding back. She was waiting for the perfect moment to make her approach. When the bell rang, the Three Musketeers hastily stubbed out their sneaky cigarette and sloped off towards the double doors that led to the main school corridor.

'Hello Billy,' teacher Pamela Smart had just caught up with the boy.

Bill was slightly embarrassed in front of his pals. It was all very well talking about women, but it wasn't so easy when they confronted you head on.

He had met Pamela Smart for the first time the previous evening when she ran a self-esteem class for teenagers from the school. She seemed so mature and adult to Bill – even though there was only five years between them. He had found himself glancing incessantly at her legs as she leaned against the teacher's desk in that classroom the night before. She had good legs for a teacher. Even a pretty face with a fashionable streaked blonde hairstyle.

He had tried to make out her breasts beneath her loose fitting knitted jumper, and when he lay in bed that night, Billy thought about those brief glimpses of her upper thighs. It might not have been reality but then he knew, from her wedding ring, that she would never become anything more than a figure to put in that memory bank, which can provide the perfect fantasy on demand.

Now, here she was approaching him in the playground.

'Will you please come to my office after school Billy. It's important,' she said almost coldly. Pamela Smart then walked off in the opposite direction.

The other two Musketeers were sniggering.

'Hey. Billy baby. Maybe it'll be your lucky night!' They were amused by the use of the name 'Billy', as opposed to the macho 'Bill'. But that adolescent theory on why she wanted to see Bill seemed a far fetched notion at the time. His thoughts were completely opposite to those of his friends. He was furious that he was going to have to stay on at school. He never liked to spend a moment longer than was absolutely necessary inside those four grey walls.

But he was puzzled all the same. She had offered no explanation. Just a direct order. It was as if she didn't want to hear any reply. He just had to obey. It was as simple as that.

Pamela's office at Winnacunnet High School was hardly a grand affair. Surrounded with shelves crammed with schoolbooks, it consisted of a table and two chairs – just enough space for her to type undisturbed.

As media studies teacher at the school, she was afforded the luxury of her own office, because she had other duties besides teaching. They included the onorous task of writing and then distributing press releases to the local newspaper and television stations about certain school events.

It was a relentless battle. And there were times when Pamela really wondered why she bothered. So little of her material was ever acted upon. She had landed the teaching job thanks to her own virtually obsessive knowledge of the media. And this was one of the drawbacks.

It was her work as a DJ on a local heavy rock station, that had sparked off her interest. She regularly indulged herself by playing her own special brand of really loud, raucous music to an audience of listeners who really appreciated her efforts. It was a part-time, unpaid job. But just to get the chance to play her favourite band Van Halen over and over again was reward in itself. It was her way of turning the clock back to her teenage years. Something she seemed to be doing more and more.

The staff at the radio station particularly enjoyed

Pam's visits, because she always went to great effort to wear really sexy clothes – like skin tight jeans and lots of leather.

Pam loved the heavy thudding bass lines and the screaming vocals. Heavy metal music made her feel really good if she was down. She idolised Van Halen in every way possible. She would have done anything to meet them in person.

Pam also had a softer, more charitable side to her nature in sharp contrast to her passion for those brutal heavy metal sounds. She used to be happy to help out at the school by teaching to the school's self-esteem programme for teenagers. After all, she herself had only just come out of her teens and she knew just what it was like. She got a real buzz out of helping the kids to discover themselves. It was a vital part of the growing up process as far as she was concerned.

The past few months had been a time of great upheaval for Pam. The previous May she had married her college sweetheart, Greg. They had moved into a comfortable apartment in nearby Derry, New Hampshire. But, as a salesman, he was often away and she found it difficult being on her own at home so often, with only the dog for company. That was another reason why she had volunteered to teach the programme.

In the class that previous evening, she had clearly noticed Bill Flynn studying her body. She did not think Bill noticed the wry smile that came to her lips at that moment. Maybe it was just as well.

It was hardly a new experience for Pam. As a young female teacher, a lot of the boy pupils would lust after her. Imagining what they would like to do to her. Stripping her with their eyes. Fantasising about bedroom encounters.

It amused her. When she was a pupil at school herself, she had always been the girl who would flirt in the playground. She used to love teasing them by leaving a button undone or pursing her lips. It was fun. So good for one's confidence. She missed the attention she used to get from all those boys. It just wasn't the same once you had grown up. People expected you to behave more responsibly. You could no longer act wild.

Pam would often flashback to those days when she found herself jealously watching the kids in the playground at Winnacunnet doing exactly the same thing. She wished she could do it all over again.

When Pam spotted Billy in the playground that morning, she felt compelled to do something. He was such a nice looking boy with that mane of dark wavey hair and those sea blue eyes. She had watched as he and his friends flirted with that blonde schoolgirl on the other side of the playground. She wanted Bill to notice her and flirt with her – but he didn't.

Now she had him all to herself here in her office.

'Sit down Billy,' said Pamela, as the teenager stepped nervously into the room.

Bill was still puzzled. He could not quite work out why Pamela had made him stay late. Maybe she had noticed him leering at her the previous evening and wanted to reprimand him? If that was the case, he felt highly embarrassed. It was all very well thinking those dirty thoughts but he didn't want to be confronted with them by the object of his fantasies.

Few words passed between them before she produced an envelope and gave it to him. He did not question why. But just opened it.

'I hope you like them,' was all she said.

It was clear from the package they were family snap shots. Perhaps she was trying to relax him by showing him pictures of her family before she punished him. Bill was very confused. What on earth was she handing them to me for? he wondered.

'Go on. Go ahead and look,' insisted Pamela.

Before opening the package, Bill hesitated for a moment. None of this made any sense. It was ridiculous.

He was about to ask why when Pam repeated 'Go on. Open it.' He felt compelled to do as he was told. As he took the snapshots out of the packet, he froze. His eyes were feasting upon the photograph on top of the pile. Bill was speechless. Stunned by the contents. He could not believe what was happening.

Picture after picture showed Pamela in just the way he had dreamt about her the previous evening.

But she had an even better figure. He did not realise teachers could have such fantastic bodies.

She was wearing the briefest of bikinis in every shot. But it was the look on her face that said it all, loud and clear. She had a sensual gleam in her eyes. They said: 'Come here. I want you.' For a moment, he wondered if these were taken just before she had sex. All the evidence seemed to point to that conclusion.

Her body was far more sensational than it could ever seem in the classroom. His pals would not believe him if he told them.

Bill was having trouble keeping his hands from shaking. He was still bewildered. Here he was sitting in a teacher's office at school while she showed him the sexiest set of pictures he had ever seen in his life. They might not have been as graphic as the soft porn mag he had flicked through at a friend's house only a few days previously, but this was a real person – not some dolly girl whose name in the captions probably did not even exist. The model in this case was sitting opposite him in that very room.

Pam was watching his reaction with interest. She could see him fidgeting uncomfortably in his seat. She wanted him to relax. She knew she was going to have to lead the way. She wondered if he really was a virgin after all. Somehow, she thought, he was.

She stood up and walked around to the side of the desk where Bill was sitting. He looked at her in a daze, unable to cope with what was happening. The photos still clutched in his clammy hands.

She knew he was bewildered. It was exactly how she wanted him. She wanted to be the dominating force. Leading the way with every move. Only deciding what she wanted to do. He just had to obey her.

Then she leant against the desk in exactly the same way she had done on the previous night. It was a deliberately provocative act. She wanted an excuse. She needed to have that control over him.

She kept repeating the lines to her favourite Van Halen song Hot For Teacher. It was all about the seduction of a pupil by his teacher.

Pam wriggled her hips ever so slightly to losen up the tight fitting skirt she was wearing. Bill was at last beginning to realise that his teacher had seen every one of his reactions the previous evening. She had obviously enjoyed every glance. Now he had an extraordinary opportunity to translate those fantasies into reality.

Pam stroked his hair gently. Touching and probing with one hand. The other traced circles around the inside of his ear lobe. Then she picked up the photos and handed them to Bill. 'Find the one you like best.'

To Bill, every picture was too hot to handle. They were all as suggestive as each other. He wasn't interested in the pictures. He wanted the real thing.

'You've got to pick out the best one Bill,' she repeated her request. But, by now, it had become an order. Bill showed her a shot of her on all fours taken from behind. It was an incredibly provocative photograph.

On the day she posed, Pam had been determined to act as sexily as possible – twisting her body in a way that would maximise her ultimate message to whoever she showed them to. As her best friend Tracey Collins took the photos, she kept repeating: 'Do you think they are sexy enough? Tell me they are. Tell me they are.'

She hoped it would turn on her husband Greg. But, instead, he was appalled and demanded that she destroy the pictures. He craved respectability not all this sordidness.

'Well if he doesn't like the pictures I'll find someone else who will,' she thought to herself.

Now she was about to put those pictures to the test by using them to seduce a 15-year-old boy.

Bill sat there in her office, still drifting in and out of reality. At one point he decided it must all be a dream. His mind began to wander. Then he felt Pamela's hand stroking and caressing. It was all becoming very real once more.

Suddenly, Pamela pulled her hand away from Bill's lap. She had heard voices outside the door to her office. Bill came to. Snapped out of his sexual trance. Perhaps taking a split second longer to register the disturbance nearby.

'Don't worry Billy. You'll have me next time,' she whispered.

Next day found Billy wandering around the playground in a trance of disbelief. Had she really shown him those photos? His fellow musketeers were worried. 'What's wrong Bill? You ill or something?' Vance said.

Bill's mind was elsewhere.

He could not stop thinking about her. The chance to break his virginity had been so close and yet so far last night. But at least he now had a chance to actually lose it with a real woman – not some giggling classmate with as little experience as him.

The strange aspect was that Bill also felt a great deal of affection for Pamela. He didn't see her as a grand seducer only interested in satisfying her own sexual desires. Rather, he portrayed her as a beautiful woman who actually wanted him for more than just his young, lithe body.

It was for that reason Bill decided to break his code of friendship within the Three Musketeers and not tell them about his encounter with her – for the time being at least. If she ever found out that he'd been blabbing he'd lose his chance for good.

Across the other side of the playground, Pamela was watching and waiting once more. This time Bill noticed her instantly. That delighted her. She wanted that attention – and now she was getting it.

Minutes later, in the corridor, she touched his arm gently and said: 'Come to my home tonight.' She passed him a scrap of paper with her address. The appointment was set. It was now only a matter of time.

Bill was ecstatic.

Pamela had been planning this moment in her mind for a long time. She was fed up with those lonely nights in front of the TV screen with only her mongrel dog for company. She had kept asking Greg to change jobs so he could be around more. But, as he continually explained to her, it was not that easy. She was resigned to spending at least half the nights of the year alone. Once a week, she would host the heavy rock radio show. That was real fun. She adored the music and people at the station. They all seemed to have a much better life than her.

But the rest of her life seemed painfully empty.

When she had first met Greg at that teenage party, all those years ago, he had seemed just like her. With his shoulder length hair and love of heavy metal music they seemed to have so much in common. Both loved nights out with their mutual friends.

Greg looked like Jon Bon Jovi, and behaved like him sometimes. She liked that badness in him then. It was such a happy time for Pamela. She used to love dressing up in her heavy metal studded leather jackets and skirts, often adding fishnet stockings – oozing sex to all around her but still retaining a one-woman one-man passion for Greg. At rock concerts around the entire country, they and their friends would head bang to the hypnotic sounds, like millions of other teenagers.

Then Greg took a job as an insurance salesman

and cut off all his long locks. He wanted to turn the clock forward and grow up. Pamela wanted to stay young and carefree.

Calling herself the Maiden of Metal, she took on the part-time job at the radio station and kept playing her Van Halen tracks. She began to think more and more about their message. They would always be her inspiration.

While Greg was settling down, with a safe career and a nice home, she was still firmly anchored in a teenage world of heavy metal, wild friends and all night parties.

Only a few weeks earlier, they had had an awful row when Greg announced he was going skiing with some friends. Pam was furious. How could he leave her alone after all those nights he had been away for work? They really screamed at each other that night. She even told Greg she wished they'd never got married.

'You've just become some boring yuppie. You're not the man I married.'

To Greg, it was a painful insult. He retaliated in a crushing outburst and poured out the details of a sordid one night stand he had had some weeks earlier.

Pam was horrified. She felt betrayed. But that feeling turned to anger when he explained: 'I was really drunk at the time. I didn't know what I was doing.'

In her eyes, that was no excuse. From that day on

her hated for him grew like a cancer, gnawing away at her insides.

Now she waited for her 15-year-old virgin pupil to arrive so she could give him her lessons in love. Just the mere thought of what she would do to Bill excited her as she waited there in the modest two-bedroomed apartment.

She had planned it all with great precision. Greg had hurt her. Now she was intending to get her revenge. Earlier that evening, she went to the video store to rent Nine and a Half Weeks. Pamela had seen it once before with husband Greg. They had both found it a real turn on. Now she was hoping it would have the same effect on Bill. Even the fridge was filled with beers to guarantee that the teenager would feel completely in the mood.

The stage was set. It just needed the other player.

The other player was feeling very nervous. The air of expectancy that he had felt earlier had now dissolved into a very real masculine fear that he might not be able to perform. After all, he had never had sex before in his young life. What happened if he climaxed too soon? How would he know what parts of her body were the most sensitive? He knew she would have to lead him and educate him.

As he rang the door bell something inside him half wished she wouldn't be there. Then he could just turn round and walk home. Escape the embarrassment of not being experienced. He genuinely feared that she thought he had slept with at least three or four women already.

But Pam was only too well aware of his limitations. It pleased her to think that she was going to teach him so much. It made her feel wonderful that she could influence every aspect of their relationship. She had complete power over him. Perhaps even enough power to persuade him to carry out the ultimate sacrifice?

As she opened her front door she felt a surge of excitement rushing through her body. She knew he was hungry to learn – and she wanted so badly to be his teacher. Bill also felt an instant rush of adrenaline. But it was for a different reason from her. In those few moments it took her to open the door, his attitude had undergone a complete about-turn. His guilt had evaporated. He was now desperate to have her. This was going to be it. All those fears about sex had been stupid. Now he just wanted it. Wanted it really badly.

Pam's medium length hair was no longer tied back. Instead she had it falling neatly around her face. The make-up was more elaborate than at school. Her lips were glossed. They had seemed thin before. Now they were much fuller. Enveloping. Coaxing. She licked her top lip. Her tight fitting skirt was much further above the knee than any skirt she had worn to school. She was wearing flesh coloured tights, or were they stockings? He was desperate to find out. He could see just a hint of her bust and a bra through the opened top three buttons of her blouse.

Pam and Bill were not even inside the apartment yet. But the atmosphere was clearly sexually charged.

That much was patently obvious to Pamela's friend Cecilia Pierce. She was sitting on the settee in the lounge when the couple walked in from the hallway.

Bill was taken aback. He had not expected to see Cecilia here. Perhaps he'd got it all wrong? Maybe Pam's behaviour the previous night was just a tease? How could she invite a friend along when she was planning the great seduction. It just did not make sense. A look of obvious disappointment came over Bill's face. Both women could see it clearly.

'Hey. Billy,' said Pam. 'I got a really hot movie for us all to watch.'

But Billy wasn't listening. His mind was racing ahead. Either he had imagined the incident in the office or perhaps he was going to end up with both these women tonight? What an experience that would be, he thought.

Soon, all three were sitting back, transfixed by the video of Nine And A Half Weeks.

Basinger's character Elizabeth begins the film by rejecting sex-mad Rourke, saying: 'You're taking a hell of a lot for granted.'

In Pam's sitting room that evening, Bill was just praying he could.

But, back on celluloid, it wasn't long before Rourke got his woman in a sex scene that is said to have been one of the steamiest in Hollywood history.

Bill watched open mouthed as Rourke's character 'John' blindfolded 'Elizabeth'. Perhaps that's what Pam wanted to do to him?

The atmosphere in the sitting room was expectant, to say the least. All three were transfixed as 'John' took an ice cube out of a glass of whisky and began dripping drops of ice cold water onto Elizabeth's body. Then he rubbed the cube over her lips before sensuously stroking the beautiful actress's nipples. Finally, he traced the edge of her panties with an ice cube between his teeth.

It was an outrageous scene, deliberately scripted to give maximum titilation to the audience. It was certainly having the desired effect on the three watching.

Pam was already planning precisely how she would make Bill re-enact the film in her bedroom. As Kim Basinger performed a really hot striptease as part of yet another seduction scene with Mickey Rourke, Bill hoped Pam would do the same for him later on. At one stage, Kim become Pam as his imagination began to work overtime.

They they watched spellbound as Mickey Rourke ravaged Kim Basinger up against a wall in a street. Torrents of water cascaded over the two stars as they tried at least six different positions.

'Wow. He's got a great body,' both the girls were giggling in schoolgirl fashion as the camera followed the contours of Rourke's body.

Bill looked away embarrassed for a moment by the naked male form. But soon his eyes were once more glued to the TV set, as Basinger's figure was exploited to the full.

It was clearly one of Pam's favourite movies. She fidgeted and crossed, then uncrossed, her legs throughout. Her tight skirt rode higher and higher up her thighs. She knew it was happening but she did not care. She could feel the rush of cool air going between her legs.

Bill knew that if he had to stand up it would be embarrassing because of his huge erection. He looked over toward Pam. He could clearly see her stocking tops and the contrasting bare flesh above. At that moment, they watched Basinger – dressed in black stockings and figure hugging pencil skirt masturbating while she fantasised over Rourke.

Earlier that day, Pamela had informed Cecilia she was inviting the youngster round, telling her in no uncertain terms that she wanted to have the boy. But she wanted Cecilia to pretend to be his girlfriend if anyone called round unexpectedly. The irony was that Cecilia was nearer to his age – she was just 16. But she realised that Pam needed to have her around as cover in case Greg got back from a skiing trip early. It certainly would not do if he walked in on Pam and Bill alone. Greg was a jealous man.

'It must be giving you a few ideas Bill.' The movie was almost over but the real action was only just beginning as far as Pam was concerned.

On the screen, Basinger was walking away from Rourke, having rejected one of his perverse requests for the last time. She had decided they had to finish before it was too late.

As the end credits rolled, Pamela got up and went into the kitchen. Cecilia smiled knowingly. She knew she was playing the extra on this occasion. But it did not bother her.

Bill was lost for words. He just hoped this was all going to lead to what he had earlier envisaged. The sexy message of the movie was loud and clear. But where did Cecilia fit in?

Pamela swiftly answered that when she returned from the kitchen with a tray of ice cubes and took his hand.

'Let me show you the rest of the apartment ...'

Bill just couldn't believe it was finally actually happening. All this expectation and now they were really doing it.

Pamela was firmly in control. Bill knew his place the instant she peeled off her skirt and blouse to reveal a turquoise set of silk lingerie.

As she undid the belt of his trousers, he felt like her pupil once more. It was a nice, secure response. He was unsure. He wanted to be led. She seemed so powerful. So strong. He just did as he was told.

In the first few moments, Bill was embarrassed by

his own nudity. But he soon shed his inhibitions as Pamela explored every part of his body in the dimly lit bedroom.

The partly empty ice cube tray was on the bedside table. Bill had smothered the freezing cold pieces all over her body. He was fascinated by the erectness of her nipples when he touched them with the cubes.

He was pushing them gently over every curve, then licking the watery remains with his tongue in a really teasing fashion. It was driving Pamela into spasms of excitement. It was the only time Bill ever got anywhere near being in complete control.

He stopped to put the ice cubes back in the tray, desperate to actually make love. He understood the importance of foreplay but he really wanted the real thing. Each time he tried to stop though, she would insist he carry on with the ice cubes. She wanted him to put them in her mouth and drip tiny droplets onto her body just like in the movie.

It was time for Cecilia to go. She could well imagine what was going on in the bedroom next door. She had to pass the bedroom door to get out of the apartment, so she braced herself. It wasn't that she was shocked by Pamela's seduction technique. More jealous really.

For Cecilia had been equally turned on by the movie, but she had no one to turn to. As she crept past the door, that was ever so slightly ajar, she could clearly see the two naked bodies entwined and heaving on the double bed. It was an image she would never forget.

At last Bill was discovering the real thing. They were making love on the bed wildly and rampantly, totally consumed by each other's bodies.

It was a brilliant experience. Sex with an older, more experienced woman!

Pamela's appetite for lust knew few boundaries. She was training her 'love slave' to do anything she demanded.

In the background, Van Halen's Hot For Teacher was blaring out of the stereo system. Reminding Pam of her conquest. How could she ever forget?

Now she wanted sex on the floor. He had to obey as she pulled him on top of her, guiding him into her because he was still clumsy and inexperienced.

As their bodies moved in rhythm on the shag pile carpet, she fantasised about Mickey Rourke. She knew she would reach a climax, just so long as Bill was half as good as Mickey was.

Bill was feeling guilt-ridden. It was a classic schoolboy guilt. He wasn't sure if he could face Pam again after their night of passion. Now he had actually experienced sex, he was not quite sure how to handle it. Should he ignore Pam and hope her husband does not find out? Or would it be better to take the affair a stage further and become her regular lover?

He could not believe that a woman would give herself to him in the way Pam had, without feeling very emotionally involved. He had read about prostitutes and sex on demand. But Pam was not like that. There was only one conclusion to draw: something special must exist between them.

As he stood in his regular place in the corner of the school playground on the morning after he lost his virginity, he felt a strange combination of elation and depression. The joy of that sexual experience was being mellowed by the ongoing feeling of guilt.

But then he snapped out of it when he sensed Pam's eyes upon him from the other side of playground. This time she was coming towards him, rather than holding back by the double doors like before. As she approached, the other two Musketeers moved away, instinctively aware of the relationship between their best friend and his teacher. Pam had been rehearsing this moment all morning. Now the time had come.

Bill did not know where to look at first. Pamela had obviously been crying. The mascara around her eyes had smudged and she looked a different person from the passionate vamp of just a few hours earlier.

They talked in low, almost whispered tones, to avoid the prying ears of the other children standing nearby.

'I want you so badly Billy,' uttered Pamela.

Bill did not know what to say. She was proclaiming her love for him.

'I've got to have you the whole time. I don't want anyone else. I want you.'

Pamela was weeping slightly throughout, but she still had that air of authority about her. The teacher in charge. There was no way he could refuse her anything. If she wanted just him and no one else than that was fine by him.

There was something wrong though. She seemed to be building up to it. As if she had some other motive for her tears ... but he couldn't be sure of it. It did not take long for him to find out.

'We've got to get rid of Greg. It's the only way.' Bill reeled back with shock. Maybe he wasn't hearing her correctly? But Pamela was being deadly serious. She wanted Greg out of the way and she ordered Bill to do it.

The car was parked in a narrow lane off the main highway. It was eight o'clock in the evening. The windows were heavily steamed up and the car was gently rocking – only slightly – from side to side. It was just enough so you would notice if you were standing right by it.

Inside, Pamela and Bill were making love. It wasn't as comfortable as the first time. But it was just as passionate.

'Bill. If you really loved me ...'

Pamela wanted her young lover to prove his commitment to her. Bill was in a daze. He had just turned 16 years of age, and now his married girlfriend was briefing him on how to kill her husband. In between gasps she said:

'Make it look like a burglary. Steal a few thing from the bedroom ... There's some jewellery in there ... The cops will think Greg walked in on the burglars ... It's going to be so simple ... I don't want you to do a messy job. It's got to be clean and quick ... Use a gun then you won't mess up the carpet.'

She was ordering the assasination of her husband but her chief concern was her new lounge carpet.

'And don't do it in front of the dog. I don't want him scared.'

Pam always said she preferred animals to humans – now she was proving that point beyond any doubt.

Despite reservations Bill was getting what he always wanted – real sex from a woman who really knew how to perform. If he had to carry out certain, well, unsavoury tasks then so be it.

He wanted his lessons to last forever.

Vance Lattime was tip-toeing silently down the stairs of his home, desperate not to wake the rest of the family. As he made his way across the lobby to his father's study, he wondered if what he was about to do was really going to be worth it.

Only a few hours earlier, his best friend and fellow Musketeer Bill Flynn had persuaded him and Patrick Randall to carry out the cold blooded murder of Pamela's husband Greg.

She had been with all three of them when the plan had been discussed. She made them believe it would all be so simple. Vance was not so sure. But Bill and

Pam were most persuasive. They knew that Vance's father had a vast collection of firearms at his home.

As the teenager gently opened the glass case and eased the .22 pistol out, he hesitated for a moment. For the price on Greg Smart's head was a mere £2,400 each. That was the amount Pamela had promised Bill that he and his friends would receive from Greg's life insurance. The only condition was that they made sure he was dead.

As he stood inspecting the daunting array of weaponry on display, Vance knew he had made The Musketeers' pledge of honour – and that meant he was committed.

Bill, Vance, Patrick and their driver Ray Fowler were motoring up the freeway towards Derry. They were visibly nervous. They were having to face the reality of the situation – and it was terrifying them. As Ray drove, Bill briefed the other three on the roles they had to play.

No one was listening properly. Their powers of concentration were all but gone. These were not cold, professional killers; these were four schoolkids who had come under the spell of one determined seductress.

'Shit. Let's turn around,' Bill was back in control. Thinking clearly for a moment, he realised the enormity of their task. He could see the ludicrous side of the situation and it was time to take stock of it all. Time to reassess his true feelings for Pamela. Perhaps she was using him to kill her husband?

Maybe she would just drop him like a stone the moment the murder was committed?

For the first time, Bill had his doubts about the relationship which had picked him up and swept him off his feet.

'I'm sorry. We just got kinda lost. I couldn't remember which street you lived in.'

It was a feeble excuse from Bill and he knew it. But it was all he could do in the circumstances. Vance and Patrick were cowering with him outside the front door to Pam's apartment. They were almost more scared of her reaction than the prospect of murdering someone.

Pamela was indeed furious.

'You don't love me. You got lost on purpose,' she was screaming at Bill, totally ignoring the presence of the other two boys.

He was frightened she was going to ditch him. That would mean the end of all that passion. But at least it might leave him with a clear conscience.

Bill was half hoping that perhaps this would be the end. He was worried about a lot of things to do with this illicit relationship. It all seemed so dangerous. So risky. But the over-riding guilt always dispersed the moment he set eyes on Pam. Remembering the love making they had enjoyed seemed to lull him into a false sense of security. It was all so easy.

She started to stroke Bill's neck. She was going to get her way. No matter what it took. The two other boys looked on embarrassingly as their media studies teacher kissed and caressed her pupil in front of their very eyes. Pam was well aware of the presence of those other two. She led Bill into the kitchen and told them to let themselves out ...

Soon they were making love all over the house. On the sitting room floor. On the staircase. And finally in the bedroom.

Pamela's initial anger at Bill had now transformed into lust. Her fury about the failed attempt on her husband's life was making her more frantic.

Bill could barely handle it. She was oozing with sex. She did not remove her clothes for the first bout of love making – not even her black patent leather stilettos.

She was tearing at him wildly. Wanting more. And more. And more.

By the time they had both climaxed, Pam was like a different person. All the anger had subsided. She had let it all flow out of her system during the love making. She felt immensely satisfied ... for the time being.

Gently, she stroked his chest and looked at him lovingly, as they relaxed together in her double bed. But that nagging feeling she wanted something was coming back to Bill. It was the same feeling that he had when they lay on the back seat of the car a few days earlier.

He knew exactly what was on her mind.

'You've got to try again. This time make it work.

If you don't, we shall have to stop seeing each other.'

The chilling reminder made Bill's stomach turn. He wanted her so badly. Before, he had hoped the whole crazy scheme would just go away.

He should have known better.

In their Derry apartment, Greg Smart was tidying up before Pamela's return from a late evening school meeting.

He wanted so desperately to make up for the confession which had so upset Pam. He knew it was wrong to have slept with someone else. It was just one of those things. He still loved Pam and he wanted to show her how much. Now, he was looking forward to a great celebration that would wipe those bitter memories out forever.

Greg was so engrossed in his thoughts he did not even notice the smash of a rear window at first.

As the three hooded figures crept through the bedroom towards the lounge, Greg was just thinking who to call next on his round up of friends for the party.

When The Three Musketeers burst in they took Greg completely by surprise.

'Take anything you want.' He wasn't going to argue with three men and a pistol.

Bill was feeling elated. The gun. The power. The power to order someone about. Just like Pam did with him. He felt in control of his own destiny for the first time in his entire life. He knew he could get Greg to do anything he wanted. Well, almost anything.

'Give us that ring scumbag.'

He wanted that ring more than anything else. He wanted it to be his forever some day.

For a few seconds, the whole scenario was reduced to a farce by Greg's response.

'If I gave it to you, my wife would kill me.' One of the other boys sniggered.

Bill and his fellow Musketers were flabbergasted. His wife wanted him dead – and he really did not have a clue.

'Just give us it.'

Bill tried to sound menacing. But to no avail. Greg was adamant.

He had just signed his own death warrant.

Bill cocked the hammer on the gun.

'Get down on your knees. Now!' yelled Bill Flynn to his lover's terrified husband.

He pointed the gun at the back of Greg's head and uttered three simple words:

'God forgive me.'

Greg Smart fell to the floor silently.

Bill and his two fellow Musketeers beat a hasty retreat

She looked stunning dressed all in black. The seamed stockings added just that hint of sexuality, at a sombre occasion. She was even wearing the same black patent stiletto's that she had kept on during her last bout of passion with Bill.

This was the funeral of Greg Smart, and his grieving widow was putting on an Oscar winning performance. Head down, she looked heartbroken as the wooden coffin was mechanically lowered into its final resting place in the ground. The so-called Maiden of Metal was melting the hearts of her family and friends, gathered around the graveside.

As they heard the priest refer to Greg's tragic death at the hands of unknown assailants, she shed a tear and dropped a bouquet of red roses onto the casket before it was covered up with earth.

'God rest his soul ...'

Back in the playground, the Three Musketeers were in a daze. They still couldn't quite believe what they had actually done.

The newspaper headlines had come and gone. Pamela Smart was still grieving at home – crying those crocodile tears. The whole operation seemed to have gone like clockwork. Now the teenagers wanted to collect their money. It seemed like a job well done.

But they were all starting to drop their guards.

The bragging at school began. Word started to get out that maybe Greg Smart wasn't killed by burglars after all.

'He was worth more dead than alive,' boasted Patrick Randall to one classmate.

It was the talk of the playground. The place where, all those months ago, the whole train of events had been set in motion.

It was now only a matter of time.

Vance Lattime was feeling really distraught. He had just woken up after having an horrific nightmare, in which he kept seeing the face of Greg Smart over and over again. It was a vivid image. Lifelike to the extreme, and it really scared the teenager.

He, more than the other two Musketeers, was constantly filled with a sense of guilt that wouldn't let go. While the other boys waited for Pamela to get in contact and hand over their 'fees', he was starting to question the whole horrific episode.

At home, his parents thought it was adolescent girl trouble that was causing Vance's depression. The problem was certainly with the opposite sex. But this was no girl. She was a murderous, manipulative woman.

His parents tried in vain to help him over his anxiety. But no amount of appeals would work.

He couldn't keep this evil secret locked up inside his mind for much longer. He knew that other kids were talking about it at school. He was sure the police would come knocking some day.

Then, one breakfast time, he snapped. Breaking down in floods of tears he poured out the entire incident to his stunned parents.

Vance's father went straight to the police.

Pamela took the news of the arrest of The Three Musketeers and their driver very calmly. She certainly was not going to be panicked into a confession.

As she sat in the once happy matrimonial home in Derry, with her best friend Cecilia, she seemed in a remarkably cool state of mind.

'Who are they going to believe? A 16-year-old, or me with my professional reputation,' she said confidently. 'I'll get off, don't worry. I'm never going to admit to the affair.'

Unluckily for Pamela, she did not notice the electronic tape recorder that was strapped to Cecilia's back ...

On March 22, 1991, at a court in Exeter, New Hampshire, Pamela Smart was found guilty of masterminding her husband's murder. She was sentenced to life imprisonment.

Bill Flynn, Patrick Randall and Vance Lattime all admitted killing Greg Smart. Their life sentences were reduced to 28 years in exchange for their co-operation in helping the prosecution of Pamela Smart.

Undying Obsession

Julia Wright had been looking forward to her holiday in the snow-capped mountains of Colorado for months. Her husband Jeremy had insisted she take a breather from the daily grind of bringing up four young children to help her sister celebrate her fortieth birthday. After almost fifteen years of marriage, it seemed like the perfect way to recharge one's batteries.

Jeremy had assured Julia that he would make sure

the children were properly looked after, even if it meant having to take time off from his busy job as a gynaecologist in the commuter-stockbroker belt of Woking, Surrey, twenty miles from London. When Jeremy first announced that he felt Julia should take the holiday she was a trifle bemused as this was not exactly a regular occurrence and she was concerned about leaving the children. However, after a series of recent 'domestic problems', it certainly seemed like a very appealing idea.

Julia flew off from Gatwick Airport on that chilly day in February 1994, not realising that her away-from-it-all trip would mark the start of a tragic set of circumstances which would end in death.

From the moment she arrived in Colorado, Julia made a point of calling home every day to see how James, aged fourteen, Julia, thirteen, Felicity, nine and Sophie, seven, were coping without their mother. She was a little surprised that Jeremy was not always in but since they had hired a home help she did not worry.

On the ski-slopes of the Rockies, Julia put the pressures of her home life behind her to enjoy some sensational downhill racing. She and her sister even managed to have actual conversations without being interrupted by the children. It was all a startling contrast with family life back in England. The holiday probably marked the first occasion in years that 46-year-old Julia had actually managed to relax, although she never put the children out of her mind for long. Like any caring mother away from her flock, she wondered if they were coping all right without her back at the house in Heath Road, Woking.

The envelope tucked neatly under Julia Wright's hotel bedroom door almost went unnoticed when she awoke for another day on the ski-slopes with her sister. As she bent down to pick it up, something inside her made her shiver momentarily. She had a bad feeling and she could not work out why.

A few seconds later her instincts were proved completely correct. Inside the envelope was a fax from husband Jeremy in England, informing Julia in clinical, almost business-like terms that he had moved out of their home and was living with his receptionist and close family friend, Mrs Fiona Wood.

Julia kept reading the fax over and over again in the hope that she had made a mistake and maybe it was all a bad dream. By the time she showed it to her sister, however, she knew it was deadly serious.

How could he do it? How could he just send her a fax effectively ending fourteen years of marriage? Julia kept asking herself those questions over and over again. Celebrities like Phil Collins, Sylvester Stallone and Julia Roberts might have reportedly used faxes to end their relationships, but not respectable middle-class doctors, surely?

There was the added factor of her husband's lover, Fiona Wood. Julia felt incredibly betrayed by forty-year-old Mrs Wood, whom, until a few months earlier, she had treated virtually as a sister. Mrs Wood had held a central role in the Wright family's life since taking up her secretarial post with Jeremy in 1986. Julia Wright had always had complete and utter trust in Mrs Wood, who had controlled the Wrights' lives even to the extent of organising their holidays. She had even helped Julia to book her trip to Colorado.

Certainly, there had been strong evidence in the past of a relationship between her husband and Mrs Wood but Julia had dismissed the romance as a passing phase and had until she received that fax – been completely confident that their marriage would survive. Even when she met Mrs Wood's husband Peter and he had told her of the affair, she had chosen to bury her head in the sand and wait patiently for it to burn itself out. Julia was determined to rescue this situation as she believed there was absolutely no need to flush fourteen years of marriage and a large happy family unit down the drain.

Jeremy had actually begun his romance with Fiona when they both went to a medical conference in Washington DC the previous year. The affair had caused a lot of stress and strain for both families even before that fax arrived in Colorado and Julia's initial response had been to start behaving very erratically. In effect, she suffered a virtual nervous breakdown because of her husband's behaviour.

Just before Christmas 1993, Julia suddenly walked out of the family home without reason. A few hours later she rang from a phone box at Hatton Cross tube station, about fifteen miles away, offering no explanation for her strange behaviour but asking to be picked up and brought home. There had been another incident when she ran out of the house barefoot and sprinted over to a neighbour's home in tears.

Then, on New Year's Day, Julia made a bizarre plea for help by attempting suicide after downing pills and driving her car at high speed at the garage doors of their home, while clutching photos of her family. The following day she also tried to gas herself in the fume-filled garage.

In hospital the day after that incident, a doctor was called and advised psychiatric admission to a special hospital. Julia kept repeating to the doctor that her life was not worth living if she could not keep her husband. There was no hatred for Jeremy, just an obsessive insistence that the family had to stay together. It was further fuelled when one of the couple's daughters let slip that Mrs Wood had taken the children to the cinema while Julia had been in hospital. How dare she take over my role as mother, thought Julia.

With all this in mind, Jeremy Wright decided to remain at the family's £500,000 detached home, which gave poor Julia the impression that he would end his relationship with Fiona Wood. Julia saw it as a victory

– she had won back her husband. She never once admonished him for having the affair in the first place. She believed that his relationship with Mrs Wood was entirely the fault of that 'other woman' who had become one of her best friends and then secretly plotted to break up her family.

By the time Julia's holiday in Colorado came around, she was convinced that things at home were back on the straight and narrow or else she would never have made the trip. She actually believed that she had saved her marriage.

Within minutes of receiving that cold-hearted fax in America, all of Julia fears, anger, resentment and fury came flooding back. Throughout all of this, she remained steadfastly loyal about her husband's actions even though others in the family considered him to be an emotional coward. Meanwhile, her incredible resentment towards Mrs Wood, the 'home-wrecker', continued to grow at an alarming rate.

Within minutes of arriving back at their home after that disastrous holiday, Julia rushed into the couple's en suite bathroom, snatched her husband's bathrobe off a door hook and starting smothering it with hugs. The tears were flooding down her cheeks. She could not lose him. She would not lose him. Nobody was going to take him away from her.

The following month – March – there was little surprise among close family and friends when Julia Wright attempted suicide for the third time. However, that particular plea for help unwittingly allowed her husband to move his mistress into the family home. For while Julia was recovering after trying to take her own life, Fiona Wood was at the Wright home looking after her lover's children. It was a situation guaranteed to inflame Julia's manic determination not to lose her husband. She also became deeply paranoid that Mrs Wood wanted to take the children away from her as well.Within days of getting back home, Julia started to make it her business to find out as much as possible about her husband's illicit affair. She wanted to know precisely when it started; how often they had been together; what Jeremy's life was like now that he had moved into a house with Mrs Wood; what sort of cottage the illicit lovers had rented in nearby Cobham. She investigated the subject in much the same way as an author researches a book.

Julia even discovered a series of endearing messages left on her husband's bleeper by Mrs Wood. They were overtly romantic and reminded her of the courtship she had enjoyed with Jeremy all those years earlier, before she had given up her job as an anaesthetist to bring up their family.

Julia also started turning up at odd hours in Jeremy's surgery – the North Surrey Laser Centre – on an industrial estate near their home. On one occasion she discovered a letter he had written to Mrs Wood, saying that he loved her more passionately than anyone else. That letter shattered all Julia's illusions. The loving sentiments expressed in the note finally convinced her that her marriage was in dire trouble. Julia had literally made herself mentally ill through the stress and anger caused by her marriage break-up. Now she had to face reality.

She had given up her career to devote herself entirely to her family. Nothing else had mattered in her life. She loved her husband beyond measure and, as she saw it, he had been taken away from her and her children by another female – a woman once known to the family as 'the lovely Fiona'.

Julia's inner turmoil was twisting her mind into a contortion of hatred. One night she paged her husband at his love nest to ask him out for dinner. When he did not even bother to reply she interpreted his lack of response as having been caused by her rival for his love. She still believed that her husband was totally faultless and told friends that she would take him back at the drop of a hat. Some tried to convince Julia to get on with her life but she wouldn't hear of it. Jeremy was her life.

The following day Julia was driving her children to school through the centre of Woking when, by complete chance, she saw her husband and his lover as they passed each other in traffic. Julia was transfixed by them. She watched their every move as her husband's car drove slowly past and what she saw made her lose control of her senses. They were chatting and laughing together as if they did not have a care in the world; as if they were the happily married couple. Julia's eyes met those of her husband's lover for a split second. She never did discover if Fiona had seen her that morning.

'Fiona was sitting in the front seat and had a horrible triumphant grin on her face,' Julia later recalled. Going through Julia's mind was that she was muscling in on her children and she wasn't going to let her take her children as well. The two pillars that supported Julia Wright's life were the love of her husband, whom she believed could do no wrong, and the love of her four children.

As Julia continued to watch her husband and his lover in the traffic that morning, she felt a surge of anger and crunched her hands tightly round the steering wheel. She convinced herself that Mrs Wood was about to take over her family as well as her husband.

A few minutes later, Julia arrived at her children's school in tears and grabbed hold of a friend's arm. She told her: 'I have just seen them together ... I cannot cope.'

After dropping the children off, Julia drove home immediately. This time she was going to do something about it. She could not sit back and watch that woman take her family away from her.

She walked straight into the kitchen, ripped open a drawer and took out a five-inch Kitchen Devil knife which she had bought just a few weeks earlier. She turned around, marched straight back out to the car and drove directly to Jeremy's private surgery in Westminster Court, Old Woking, where she knew

Mrs Wood would be working.

Julia stormed in and yelled at her husband's mistress, 'You ruined our lives!'

Fiona Wood stood by with a bemused smile on her face.

'Do you realise how many people you have hurt?' ranted Julia.

Mrs Wood just laughed and muttered, 'It's mutual.'

The last thing Fiona Wood wanted was a confrontation with her lover's wife, especially as she was well aware that Julia had been becoming increasingly deranged over the previous few months.

Now Julia was being taken to the edge once again. It did not need much to push her over. She kept thinking of the children being looked after by that woman. It was enough of an incentive.

Suddenly Julia lashed out at Mrs Wood with her fists, punching her in the face several times. Then she produced the knife. 'You will not get my children. You will not get my children.'

She uttered the words over and over again.

Suddenly Julia lunged at the face of the woman who had lusted after her husband and entrapped him. She slashed at Mrs Wood's eyes and mouth eighteen times. There was blood everywhere. As her body crumpled to the floor, Julia stabbed the life out of Mrs Wood with another seventeen wounds.

'This is what happens to trusted friends who seduce husbands and wreck marriages and families,'

Julia thought to herself. 'This was what happens to scarlet women who attend the same country church and teach at the same Sunday School while all the time scheming to have an affair with her husband.'

By the time all those thoughts had passed through her mind, there was nothing left of Fiona Wood. She was a twisted, bloodied heap on the floor of the surgery where she and her doctor lover had initiated their romance.

Mrs Wood's body was so badly mutilated that she could only be identified later through dental records.

Julia felt elated by her achievement. Now she could repair the marriage and start again. She walked out of that office with her head held high.

The only other people in the building that morning heard several short screams and then silence, with one exception.

Julia – covered in the blood of her victim – ran up the hall to her husband's consulting room. She threw open the door and rushed into Jeremy Wright's arms.

'Everything is all right now. You can come home. I have killed her. She is a wicked woman who has taken you away from your family.'

Julia Wright admitted the manslaughter of her husband's secretary and mistress, Fiona Wood, on the grounds of diminished responsibility when she appeared at the Old Bailey in December 1994. She had denied murder.

Mr Julian Bevan, defending, told the court: 'She attached no blame to her husband. She saw him as a victim. Others might not be so generous.'

'Since her arrest,' he added, she had recognised 'that her life with Jeremy is over. She did not recognise that at the time.'

Mr Bevan said he would be misleading the court if he said she expressed any remorse for Mrs Wood but she was remorseful about the consequences for her victim's family.

The judge, Mr Justice Blofeld, said he sentenced her on the basis that medical reports concluded that she was not a danger to Mr Wright or anyone else with whom he was associated.

He said she bore a 'substantial residual responsibility' and had 'no sensible reason' to act in the way she did. Julia admitted manslaughter on the grounds that depressive illness had impaired her sense of responsibility. She was jailed for four years.

Three of Julia's children were in the court to see their mother sentenced. They looked down from the public gallery as the white-faced woman, wearing a navy twin-set, was led from the dock to start her sentence in Holloway Prison. The oldest, James, waved and smiled and mouthed 'goodbye'.

The Rev James Song, former vicar of the church in Woking which the Wrights and the Woods had attended, and who conducted Mrs Wood's funeral, said after the case:

I had known Fiona Wood for about ten years and although she was a very popular person and a regular worshipper, she gave up her Sunday School teaching and her attendance at church tailed off about eighteen months before the attack. I think this was the time the affair started and she found it difficult to reconcile the two.

Wood was a hard-working, very attractive woman who lived on an estate and rose to the level of working for an eminent man – setting out his diary, running his life and organising parties and gatherings at Glyndebourne. She was given access to an affluent lifestyle.

Mr Wright had felt his marriage to have been dead for a while. She lent him a supportive ear – they talked together, then started going out for meals and from there the affair started.

She knew what she was doing. We live in the 1990s and we accept that people fall in love all the time. It is the easiest thing in the world to happen.

It [the funeral] was one of the saddest things I have ever had to do. Peter Wood was there, of course, and behind him sat Mr Wright, who had also lost someone. One of Mr Wright's children was there because they had known Fiona well.

At the end of the ceremony I was with Peter as he said goodbye to those who had attended and he shook Jeremy Wright's hand and spoke to him.

Peter behaved like the perfect gentleman. Even though their marriage had ended, the funeral fell on his shoulders. Both Peter Wood and Jeremy Wright started going to the church after the funeral. In the end the people who knew and loved Fiona were faced with the same feeling of loss.

After the case, Fiona Wood's husband Peter, a 44-year-old marketing executive, talked about his twenty years of married life with her and about their two teenage children. 'This case has brought into focus the loss that I and my family have suffered.'

He said that although he and his wife were separated at the time she was killed, they had remained on friendly terms.

He added: 'She was a lovely lady and a good friend. She was very popular.'

Jeremy Wright's mother said after the trial, 'You have to feel sympathy for someone, however deranged, who felt the need to do something so dreadful. It didn't solve any problems. The ripples it has caused are endless. No one knows where it is going to end.'

Jeremy Wright started a new relationship with another woman just six weeks after his wife killed his mistress. He has not spoken to Julia Wright since the attack.

His solicitor, defending his client's decision to start another affair so soon after the tragedy, said: 'I understand there has been criticism of him but he does not wish to answer that. He is simply interested in getting on with his life. What people think is not important.'

ALREADY AVAILABLE FROM BLAKE'S TRUE CRIME LIBRARY

DEADLIER THAN THE MALE
Ten true stories of women who kill
Wensley Clarkson

IN THE COMPANY OF KILLERS
True-life stories from a two-time murderer
Norman Parker

THE SPANISH CONNECTION
How I smashed an international drugs cartel
John Lightfoot

DOCTORS WHO KILL
Terrifying true stories of the world's most sinister doctors
Wensley Clarkson

DEADLY AFFAIR
The electrifying true story of a deadly love trial
Nicholas Davies

THE FEMALE OF THE SPECIES
True stories of women who kill
Wensley Clarkson

WOMEN IN CHAINS
The stories of women trapped in lives of slavery
Wensley Clarkson

THE MURDER OF RACHEL NICKELL
The truth about the tragic murder on Wimbledon Common
Mike Fielder

VIGILANTE!
One man's war against major crime on Britain's streets
Ron Farebrother with Martin Short

CAGED HEAT
An astonishing picture of what really goes on behind the walls of women's prisons
Wensley Clarkson

SUNDAY BLOODY SUNDAY
A chilling collection of tales from the News of the World's Sunday Magazine
Drew Mackenzie

BROTHERS IN BLOOD
The horrific story of the two brothers who murdered their parents
Tim Brown and Paul Cheston